SERVING JESUS *without* BURNING OUT

"Serving Jesus is a Christian's greatest privilege. However, it is a calling filled with challenges, trails, and opposition. Without an authentic and genuine relationship with the Savior lived out in community, burn out and drop out may keep us from finishing race well. My friends and colleagues, Scott Hildreth and Steven McKinion, are very much aware of this danger and have written a theologically rich and practical masterpiece to help us finish our race for the glory of King Jesus. I love it! I will be placing this book in a lot of hands."

—**Daniel Akin**, president, Southeastern Baptist Theological Seminary

"McKinion and Hildreth issue a clear call to those tired from the unique strains of ministry to go to the source of our strength: the Lord Jesus Christ. Every pastor should read, recommend, and revisit this work often to be reminded that the source of our strength flows from the very life of God himself, which is given to us through Christ by the Spirit. After all, it's his work, and our work is to rest in him."

—**T. Andrew Brown**, senior pastor, First Baptist Church, Starkville, Mississippi

"The success of the local church's mission rests on the health of its leaders. Tragically, however, it seems that almost every day we hear stories of men and women leaving ministry because of burn-out or moral failure. The crisis is reaching epic proportions, and our mission is suffering. *Serving Jesus Without Burning Out* offers biblically rooted wisdom for lifelong, evergreen, highly fruitful ministry. As Robert Murray M'Cheyne famously said, when it's all said and done the greatest gift we can give to our people is a consistent life of holiness."

—**J.D. Greear**, pastor, The Summit Church, Raleigh-Durham, North Carolina

"When the statistics of burn out in ministry become faces you recognize and stories you know, then the need for guidance proves urgent. Steve and Scott fill that gap and provide not only biblical wisdom from ministry experience but also a straight-shooting resource from pastors for every Christian. In these pages, they diagnose the potential dangers of ministry and chart a course forward for spiritual growth. This is the right book for this time, and it's the right book for you."

—**Stephen Lorance**, pastor of leadership development, Two Cities Church, Winston-Salem, North Carolina

"Written with wisdom and compassion, this book is an invitation to pause, reflect, and consider the deeper challenges of ministry. Every man and woman serving in vocational ministry desires to do so faithfully and fruitfully. Those same people would also tell you that while it is a gift, the wear and tear of ministry allows burnout to show up as an uninvited dinner guest. This book is a timely warning and a needed source of refreshment for anyone laboring in ministry—pastors, missionaries, teachers, counselors, and others."

—**Gregory Mathias**, associate professor of global missions, New Orleans Baptist Theological Seminary

"I receive calls on a regular basis from ministry leaders who have either made the decision to walk away from ministry or who are contemplating leaving the ministry. In those moments a resource like *Serving Jesus without Burning Out* will be incredibly helpful. Whether it is a misunderstanding of the nature and practice of ministry, a misplaced priority, or a failure to recognize one's own need for ministry friendships, this book addresses many of the most common pitfalls of burnout in ministry. I am thankful for this ministry guidebook written by two ministry leaders that I count as both friends and colleagues. Hildreth and McKinion not only write about these important principles, but they also live them out in busy ministry contexts. Whether you are just starting out or have been in ministry for decades, get a copy of this book. You will be refreshed and reminded of foundational principles that will help you last in ministry."

—**Steven P. Wade**, professor of pastoral theology, Southeastern Baptist Theological Seminary

SERVING JESUS *without* BURNING OUT

Faithful
MINISTRY
for the Long Haul

D. SCOTT HILDRETH & STEVEN A. McKINION

B&H
ACADEMIC®
BRENTWOOD, TENNESSEE

Serving Jesus without Burning Out: Faithful Ministry for the Long Haul

Published by B&H Academic®
Brentwood, Tennessee

ISBN: 978-1-0877-8708-4

Dewey Decimal Classification: 253
Subject Heading: CLERGY\ MINISTRY\ PASTORAL THEOLOGY

Cover design by Kristen Ingebretson. Cover image by Shutterstock

Printed in the United States of America
30 29 28 27 26 25 VP 1 2 3 4 5 6 7 8 9 10

We dedicate this to the pastor who shaped our view of serving Jesus, Dr. Sid Sample. Dr. Sample was faithfully serving Christ and His Church late into his 80s, leading people to know and follow Jesus Christ.

CONTENTS

Acknowledgments xi

Preface xiii

Introduction 1

Chapter 1 A Biblical Model of Ministry 7

Chapter 2 The Sustaining Power of Your Call 31

Chapter 3 Being God's Servant Where You Are, as You Are 55

Chapter 4 Lifelong Growth for Lifelong Ministry 77

Chapter 5 God's Not the Only One with a Plan for Your Life 99

Chapter 6 Workaholics Don't Die Winners; They Die Empty 117

Chapter 7 Ministry in Community 137

Chapter 8 The People Are the Ministry 155

Eight-Week Challenge 171

General Index 189

Scripture Index 197

Acknowledgments

In many ways, this book is the result of decades of learning, growing, maturing, and serving. Between us, we have served in ministry for over sixty years. For the last twenty-six years (for Steve) and the last fifteen years (for Scott), we have not only served in ministry, but have served through training for ministry at Southeastern Baptist Theological Seminary. We are thankful to God and the seminary for that opportunity.

We are also thankful to the churches we currently serve. Scott is an elder at Summit Church in Raleigh-Durham. Steve is Pastor of Preaching and Vision at Woodland Baptist Church in Wake Forest. The people in our respective churches give us the opportunity day in and day out to serve Jesus. They make the work of the ministry a lighter load than it might otherwise be. They encourage and bless us greatly. Our prayer is that this book will be a resource for the staff members we are privileged to serve alongside to help them develop the foundation for a lifetime of faithful and fruitful ministry. Their encouragement is a tremendous source of strength.

To everyone who reads this book that is currently struggling: we understand. Both of us have had hard seasons of ministry. Sometimes those seasons were due to poor decisions, sometimes to ignorance, sometimes to other people acting unwisely, and sometimes due to difficult circumstances in life. There is often pain in ministry. It is hard to minister to people. But even in times of struggle, God proves himself to be faithful. Time and again the amazing grace of God, extended to us in Jesus Christ and known by the power of the Holy Spirit, grants us the strength to proceed. For that, we are most thankful.

We pray that this book encourages, equips, corrects, and inspires to love and good works.

Preface

I (Steve) have the privilege of serving as pastor of a local church. It is a great delight to preach the gospel to a family of believers week after week, to lead staff meetings, to equip leaders, and to point people to the glorious truths of God's work in Christ found in the Scriptures. The joys of ministry often stand alongside significant challenges. The responsibility of leading a congregation of believers can sometimes be overwhelming. We both know the same is true for any area of ministry, whether serving as a pastor, elder, Bible study teacher, children's minister, or even a missionary in a difficult location. Both of us have, at various times, served as a pastor, a church staff member, a missionary, and a seminary professor. And there is one universal truth in every context: ministering to people is not easy.

The relational nature of ministry is perhaps the greatest cause of burnout. Knowing the challenges you face as a minister because of people can help you address those challenges and avoid the causes of burnout and failure in ministry. What are some of the personal challenges ministers face that contribute to frustrations, which often lead to burnout?

Emotional Pressures

One of the most significant frustrations pastors face is the emotional investment they must make in the lives of their church members. The pastoral ministry is inherently emotionally demanding, requiring pastors to navigate the highs and lows of their congregants' lives. Celebrating joys, mourning losses, and providing solace during crises takes an emotional toll on pastors. Additionally, ministers carry the burdens of so many people on their shoulders that they often become overwhelmed. Ministering to people can become emotionally exhausting. To avoid this exhaustion, the pastor must find a balance that allows him to be sympathetic and empathetic without being crushed by the weight of the emotional aspects of ministry. A good place to start in finding that balance is to recognize some sources of emotional exhaustion.

Mourning with Those Who Mourn

The church is filled with people who will suffer loss and grief. Death is an inevitable aspect of life. Pastors who are intimately involved in the lives of people in the church will find themselves often in the midst of great sorrow. When I was a summer youth minister in college, having served in ministry for a grand total of about a month, the pastor and his family went on a summer vacation. Just after midnight on the first night of their absence, I received a call that a young man in the church had been killed in an automobile accident. Thankfully, two deacons in the church came and picked me up to go visit with the family. I had no idea what to say. The deacons ministered to this family as I watched in horror as a mother and father mourn their son. In the last thirty-three years of ministry, I have sat with many (too many) families in their darkest moments without much to offer other than the love of God in Christ. The emotional pain of that first encounter remains with me today. Thankfully, for those who are grieving, God has given them a pastor to be with them during those times. But for the pastor, mourning with those who mourn never gets any easier. The constant exposure to grief and loss, from funerals to broken marriages to personal tragedies, can be emotionally draining. While pastors come alongside church members to offer comfort and support, they can too easily internalize the suffering, leading to their own sense of sadness. Grief and suffering can cause considerable emotional distress for pastors.

Personal Sacrifices

Your calling as a pastor is to a life of servant leadership. Self-sacrifice is a part of the job. This selfless service often requires you to put the needs of others before your own. Learning the balance of self-care, protecting yourself and your family from the emotional exhaustion that comes from juggling the demands of ministry, family, and personal well-being, can be difficult. Balancing the responsibilities of ministry without neglecting your own spiritual, emotional, and physical well-being is necessary. I have heard people say, "the devil never lets up," as if this point justifies working long hours without reasonable rest and time away. But this is a foolish attitude. Your congregation needs you to be healthy (see chapter 4) to be a good pastor for them. But, perhaps more importantly, if you have a family, they need you to be a good husband and father before you are a good pastor. You were called to be a husband and father before you were called to be a pastor. It is important to remember that while there may be another church in your future, there is not another family in your future. Churches do not always give attention to their pastor's needs, leading to frustration, anger, and broken relationships. You cannot allow your ministry to exact such an emotional toll on you that you become ineffective as a Christian, much less as a pastor. Recognize the danger posed by unnecessary personal sacrifices and find ways to balance the necessary ones with the needs of yourself and your family.

One way to make sure you are striking a healthy rhythm is to set aside time each month to evaluate your calendar. Look at the past month. Are there areas of imbalance or neglect? Look at the coming month. Here you will see commitments and appointments. What adjustments can you make to ensure you do a better job balancing your commitments? If you are struggling with this exercise, ask someone else to evaluate your schedule with you. This person will not be as emotionally attached to your schedule and may be able to give honest and helpful feedback.

Overwhelming Spiritual Burdens

Ministry is a work inherently concerned with the spiritual lives of people. Sometimes people are less interested in their spiritual formation than their pastor is. That puts an enormous burden on the pastor who has to watch, typically helplessly, while a church member suffers from foolish decisions or hurts others because of their sin. Sometimes just the weight of seeing people who refuse spiritual nourishment can be overwhelming. The weight of spiritual responsibility can become a heavy burden for pastors.

When people in the church act in ungodly ways or question the message of the Bible, pastors can struggle with doubts, spiritual dryness, or feelings of inadequacy. These frustrations may be amplified as we realize that our people continue to ignore the messages we prayerfully write and teach. These struggles often result in frustrations with the people the pastor is called to serve, again resulting in strained or broken relationships.

Lack of Boundaries

Pastors do not have set hours they work each week. A minister is never off the clock. Meetings during the day are accompanied by meetings at night. A pastor may work all day long and then have several phone calls or emails in the evening. In some ways, this is completely understandable. A church member who is working all day only has the evening to reach out to the pastor or meet with him. Pastors have to realize that ministering to people rarely happens during "office hours." This means pastors must work with their churches to create boundaries when possible.

Because the relational nature of the ministry means the pastor's work often blurs the lines between "professional" and "personal" lives, pastors struggle with setting limits on their availability. And churches may not understand this struggle, which requires good communication between the church and the pastor to prevent frustrations or disappointment. Balancing personal time while still being available to the people of the church can be a real challenge. But a pastor who wishes to be faithful must find a way to have healthy boundaries without being isolated from the congregation.

It is hard to imagine having a fruitful ministry if you are rarely available. But you are guaranteed to burn out if you do not establish healthy boundaries for yourself and your family. Being available to the congregation does not mean you become unavailable to your family and friends.

Conflict

Churches are not immune to conflict. In fact, many of the letters in the New Testament were written to churches in conflict. Jesus experienced conflict in his ministry. The apostle Paul addressed conflict in the churches he planted and ministered to. In fact, the apostles Paul and Peter had their own conflict with one another! (Galatians 2) All relationships have their own sources of conflict. Because ministry is built around relationships, it will be filled with conflict as well. Thankfully, we are reminded that God has given the ministry of reconciliation to the church, so there are solutions to the conflicts we encounter. But the conflicts are real and they pose a real challenge to the pastor's well-being in ministry.

Ministry requires us to learn to deal wisely and resolutely with conflict. When the conflict is because of sin, there must be correction. But correcting people can be exhausting and can lead to further conflict between that person and the pastor. When the conflict is due to misunderstanding or differences of opinion, the pastor can be tempted to support one person against the other. Rather than taking sides and exacerbating the conflict, the pastor must work to help the parties involved be reconciled to one another. In any case, dealing with conflict is utterly exhausting for the pastor.

The drama associated with conflict can be a considerable distraction from the work of the ministry. The pastor, however, must recognize that helping church members work through conflict is actually a part of disciple-making.

Christians must learn to be reconciled, and they also must learn to live at peace with one another. The faithful minister models this kind of peacemaking and leads the congregation in maintaining the bond of peace brought to the church by the Holy Spirit. However, conflict can be a source of considerable frustration, leading the pastor to withdraw from people in the congregation at a time when he must strive to lean into the relationship he has with those experiencing conflict. The exhaustion you may experience as a pastor due to unresolved conflict is a significant challenge to overcome.

Isolation and Loneliness

Another significant relationship challenge pastors face is loneliness. Pastors sometimes isolate themselves from the congregation because they are hesitant to share their own struggles or frustrations. Vulnerability may be perceived as weakness. Worse, vulnerability may be leveraged against the pastor in future situations. Often, pastors and their families have no real friends in the church, leading to a feeling of loneliness. The congregation may contribute to the sense of isolation, even unintentionally, by not befriending the pastor and his family. Church members may believe that the pastor has "too many" friends, leaving no time for someone else. Additionally, people in the church may only interact with the pastor about "church" matters, avoiding friendships and "normal" conversations, isolating the pastor even more. While making genuine friendships in the congregation may be hard, as is any relationship, there is much value in building authentic relationships for the pastor. When ministers face personal challenges, they too need someone to help carry their burden. In churches with a plurality of pastors, this isolation can be addressed with other staff members. But in smaller churches with fewer ministerial staff, the pastor must address the danger of isolation and loneliness in some way or risk the consequences.

Unmet Expectations

There is perhaps no greater cause of unhappiness and frustration in relationships than having unmet expectations. Starting a job with one set of expectations only to realize the job is something completely different is terribly frustrating. When two people get married they each anticipate what marriage will be like. When the reality of marriage is something other than what they anticipated it to be, they become frustrated and even angry. Pastoral ministry can be the same way. You will anticipate what your relationship with the church will be like, but the reality may not match that anticipation. As a pastor you will have certain expectations of people in the church. Church members will likewise have expectations of their pastor. You anticipate doing certain tasks as the pastor. People in the congregation may expect that you will do something different than you plan to do. When someone has unmet expectations in the ministry, whether it is the church or the pastor, frustrations are going to follow.

Both pastors and congregations suffer from having idealized visions of what ministry is supposed to be. Pastors have unrealistic expectations of their church members. They may expect members to listen to their every word, to attend every service, to volunteer for every program, to tamp down grumblings, and to be content with whatever level of care the pastor provides. The reverse is also true. Churches expect their pastors to be available at all times, to make every hospital visit, to accommodate every wish, and to have the perfect life. Pastors may become disappointed when the church does not live up to expectation. And, more importantly, they may feel overwhelmed when the church places unrealistic expectations on them. Frustration with the congregation may lead to anger. Pastors must learn to deal with these frustrations to avoid the inevitable consequences of bitterness. Navigating unmet expectations in the ministry is the same as navigating unmet expectations in any relationship. Pastors must practice genuine humility in their relationship with the church while also maintaining honest and direct lines of open communication. Failure to communicate exacerbates frustrations

Experiencing Criticism

While having a set of unmet expectations may be the most common cause of conflict in the relationship between the minister and the church, the most difficult cause of conflict to handle as a pastor hmay be facing criticism. No one enjoys criticism, even when it is well-founded. Pastors soon realize that there are a hundred people in the church who know better than he does how his job should be done.

Rarely will a week go by that the pastor does not hear from someone in the church how the pastor should change his preaching style, the music, the flowers on the stage, or the way announcements are done. People will criticize his decisions about both big and small matters. Sometimes these critiques are offered in kind ways. Other times they are offensive. Sometimes church members are truly trying to be helpful to the work of the ministry. Often, they are motivated by preferences instead. Criticism can be loving. It can also be biting. Emails that begin, "People have been complaining about . . ." are more painful than just about any other kind. Church members can be hurtful, either intentionally or unintentionally. And it is just a part of ministry.

Learning to receive criticism, even unjust criticism, with humility can be hard. Remaining self-assured in your calling while also seeing criticism as a chance to grow and mature can seem impossible. However, the pastor who wishes to have a lifelong, faithful ministry must learn to receive criticism with an attitude of openness. Taking every question of your performance or decision-making personally will only frustrate you to no end. Practicing humility does not mean that your critic is right and you are wrong. Nor does remaining humbly resolute mean you cannot learn something from your critic. Regardless of the value of the criticism or the motivation of the critic, you must expect criticism to come. Learning to handle that criticism Christianly will help you respond in ways that do not inhibit your ministry to people in the congregation, including those most critical of what you are doing or how you are doing it.

Introduction

We all know the experience. We are cruising down the interstate, making great time. But then red lights start to light the road ahead, and traffic comes to a stop. Then, as you creep along, everything just pops open, and the road ahead is clear again. You scan the area to find the issue and realize that the problem is not in your lane after all. Something happened across the way, but drivers on your side slowed down to look at things. A quick tap of the brake, then you are driving free again.

This book is that tap of the brake.

By design, it will slow you down and allow you to breathe, think, and plan. Hopefully, as you take your foot off the gas pedal of hectic ministry, you will avoid the same mistakes and life-shattering decisions that caused the wrecked ministry that so many of our fellow travelers have found themselves in. Don't assume you are immune to disaster. The person in that other lane, the one with the wrecked car (life or ministry), didn't plan on being there either.

We hope this book serves as both a warning signal and a map. Far too many of us have experienced the painful tragedy of a ministry collapse. Sometimes it is the result of giving in to temptation. Other times, the ministry falls apart because of unhealthy decisions and lifestyle choices. Regardless of the path, the end is painful for the leader and those involved in ministry. Hope is shattered, families struggle, and the name of Christ is once again associated with human failure rather than saving grace.

As seminary professors, we begin each semester reviewing the syllabus and expectations for our classes. We usually frame this discussion around the questions, Why is this class important, and how can you get the most out of it? This course introduction helps students know what to expect and how to make the best grade possible.

As we begin this journey together through the pages of this book, we need to answer three important questions:

1. What is the book about?
2. Who is the book written for?
3. How can I get the most out of these chapters?

First, this book is written to provide some tools and encouragement for avoiding and overcoming burnout in ministry. Perhaps we need to clarify a bit. We are using the word *burnout* as an umbrella term. Our concern is not only the emotional and mental exhaustion typically associated with the term. We are using *burnout* to refer to any situation that ends a ministry abruptly. This includes moral failure, deconversion, paralyzing exhaustion, and even attempts to end one's own life.

Neither of us are mental health professionals; however, it is our personal experience that most of these ministry ending events begin with unhealthy decisions and lifestyles.[1] Christian ministry is hard work; there is nothing

[1] It is possible that some readers may find themselves needing to seek help beyond that which this book can provide. While the principles in this book are designed to create healthy lives and

wrong with embracing this reality. It requires long hours and high-pressure situations. We wrote this book to help you find a healthy rhythm that makes room for God and his gospel to serve as a soul-sustaining resource as you follow his call in a broken world.

Second, this book was written for *anyone* serving in any type of Christian ministry. As we started thinking about the tragedy of burnout, it became clear that the strain of ministry is not selective. Whether you stand in the pulpit, work overseas, sit across the table from teenagers, counselees, or hurting parents, or serve behind the scenes in anonymity, you know the unique pressure of Christian ministry. It is also clear to us that the devastation caused by ministry collapse is not lessened if the minister is a man or a woman or if the person receives a salary or volunteers their time.

Even though many of the illustrations in the book may feel weighted toward the pastorate, we have tried to be balanced in our points of application. If we are going to address the crisis affecting our churches and ministries adequately, we will need to understand that each of us in ministry plays a vital role and that we are also candidates for burnout and failure.

Third, as we noted earlier, this book is designed to be a tap on the brakes. To get the most out of the book, we suggest you read each chapter in the order it is written. The book begins by challenging some common misconceptions about ministry and then progresses toward building healthy habits and lifestyles. Each chapter stands on its

---

long-term ministries, please do not view this resource as a substitute for professional help.

own; however, we designed the book so that each chapter assumes information from the previous chapters.

Chapter one and two survey the Scriptures and develop a biblical framework of Christian ministry and of the significance of God's calling. Our hope is that these chapters will provide a renewed vision for the ministry in which God has placed you. The next chapter address the importance of remembering that God has gifted and placed you in ministry for his glory and your spiritual formation. We then explore the importance of continual growth and seeking personal holiness in ministry. The final chapters warn against making ministry an idol and the importance of healthy habits, friendships, and keeping a healthy perspective on the people and ministry itself. At the end of the book, you will find two helpful tools: *The 8–Week Challenge* and *Small Group Study Guide.* These tools are designed to take you deeper into the content of each chapter and help you apply the principles to your own life.

This book can be used in a classroom setting at a school or in a church. You could also work through it with an accountability group or as part of a church staff. Of course, like any book, you can read it alone and make each section a matter of personal prayer and commitment; however, we strongly encourage you to involve others in this journey as much as possible.

Perhaps the most critical question that needs to be answered before you start reading is, Who are the authors of this book, and why should I listen to them?

Steve McKinion and Scott Hildreth currently serve as professors at Southeastern Baptist Theological Seminary in Wake Forest, North Carolina. Steve teaches theology, and Scott teaches missions. However, these statements only describe the story at the moment of this writing.

We have known each other for nearly four decades—we were part of the same youth group, were baptized in the same church, and surrendered to ministry under the same pastor. We have not always been best friends and have not always served on the same ministry team, but as we think about our lives, there has never been a time when the other was not around. The Lord has allowed us to participate in his work in various ways. We have served in American churches, on the international mission field, and now in theological education. Over the years, we have discovered the importance of friendship and accountability for ministry success and longevity.

We have walked with one another through difficult seasons of life and celebrated moments of joy. We have also watched with horror and heartbreak as friends, students, and co-workers have burned out, flamed out, or simply given up on ministry. This book is a result of years of ministry and an offering to the Lord as a simple tool for sustaining many men and women in the amazing journey of gospel ministry.

We have prayed for you, and we hope that what you read here will help you develop habits of thinking and behavior that will help you as you pursue the upward calling of God in Christ Jesus (Phil 3:14).

{ CHAPTER 1 }

A Biblical Model of Ministry

And he himself gave some to be apostles,
some prophets, some evangelists, some pastors
and teachers, to equip the saints for the work
of ministry, to build up the body of Christ,
until we all reach unity in the faith and in the
knowledge of God's Son, growing into maturity
with a stature measured by Christ's fullness.

—Eph 4:11–13

Principle: Ministry is a different type of vocation with unique challenges.

Our desire is to help you, the reader, enjoy a lifetime of faithful ministry serving Jesus. The path toward this goal is filled with pitfalls that can make life miserable for you and those closest to you. These include things like moral failings, insufficient training, physical illness, disillusionment, and beyond. In our experience, each of these problems can lead to one of the most common but neglected realities: burnout. Burnout is a frequent outcome for ministers, leading many to leave the ministry altogether. This painful experience is the result of a variety of different choices and experiences. Not only does it cause us to want to walk away, burnout can also lower our defenses and make us vulnerable to disqualifying sin. We want to help prevent the conditions for burnout in ministry, offering biblical wisdom for ministers of all types. But all of the advice we could offer would be moot if we do not start with the right understanding of what ministry is actually meant to be. We must define "ministry" if we are to fulfill the calling we have to serve in this unique vocation.

For our purposes, ministry is more than volunteering in a church activity. It is also more than being paid to do a job at a church. And while it is more than a paid position, ministry really is some *thing*. In other words, ministry is not simply doing what you do "for the glory of God." Mechanics should not dupe their customers. Lawyers cannot steal from their clients. And Christian mechanics and lawyers (like every other Christian) should seek to leverage their occupations for God's kingdom. But fundamentally, doing the work of a lawyer or mechanic is not the same thing as engaging in ministry.

Christian ministry certainly includes the congregation's care for one another, gospel proclamation to the community immediately around them, missions, worship, etc. In some ways, all that the church does is "ministry." But in this book, we are focusing particularly on that portion of the church's ministry that specifically focuses on enlisting, equipping, and empowering the members of the church to fulfill their purposes towards God, one another, and the world. This is not to narrowly define the ministry only to pastoral ministry or eldership in the congregation. All members of the church are called to minister to one another. However, there is a particular calling wherein the church identifies people in the congregation who can teach and train them to fulfill their own calling. That does include the pastoral ministry, but it also includes other leaders in the congregation as well. Bible study teachers, small group leaders, evangelism coordinators, mission trip leaders, benevolence team members, and more, are all fellow participants in the church's gospel ministry. And no one who offers leadership within the church is immune from burnout.

While in this volume we are choosing to focus more narrowly on that part of the church's mission that includes those "called out" for servant-leadership in ministry, understanding how the church's ministry is defined provides a foundation for the remainder of the book. In fact, a misunderstanding of ministry is the first cause of pastoral burnout. When pastors do not know what they are supposed to do, or, even more fundamentally, what the church is supposed to do, they can too easily labor in vain. Who wants to wake up one morning and ask, What is all of this for? Why am I spinning my wheels, neglecting my family, and wearing myself out for nothing? The minister can help avoid this feeling of purposelessness by defining "ministry" correctly.

Whether you are a seminary student training for ministry, in your first vocational ministry assignment, or in the twilight years of ministry, we want to offer a view of ministry that will give you the best chance of persevering to the end of a long and fruitful ministry to the church of Jesus Christ. In this chapter, we will describe a biblical view of the church's ministry, explain the role of the minister in fulfilling that purpose, and demonstrate the unique challenges of the ministry as a starting place for avoiding the conditions for ministry burnout. Dedicating yourself to practicing ministry in a healthy manner contributes to your own health as a minister. Whether you are a church pastor, a staff member, a volunteer ministry leader, or a missionary on the field, having a sound understanding of Christian ministry is a prerequisite for a lasting and fruitful life of serving Jesus without burning out.

What Is the Church's Mission?

Developing a model for ministering in a healthy manner starts with defining the church's mission: make disciples. A disciple is a learner, a student, a follower. A Christian is a disciple of Jesus, redeemed by the regenerating work of the Holy Spirit, forgiven of the sins that separate them from God, and given eternal life. The church exists to be a community of disciple-making disciples. Put another way, the church exists to glorify God by participating in the mission of God in the world. This mission, and the church's role within it, is presented in Matt 28:18–20, in a passage typically called the Great Commission. After his resurrection, and just before his ascension, Jesus gathered his disciples to himself and gave them a commission: make disciples of Jesus from all nations. Jesus describes this disciple-making ministry as "baptizing them [disciples] in the name of the Father and of the Son and of the Holy Spirit, teaching them to observe everything I have commanded you." New Christians are baptized into communion with the church, which serves as the place where they know the rule of Christ in their lives, are conformed to the image of Christ, grow in maturity, and learn to participate with other Christians in the Great Commission. Jesus's command to his followers is not just to make new disciples, but to teach those disciples to live faithfully as Christians, loving God and loving one another.

What Is the Church's Ministry?

The life of the Christian community is expressed through the ministry of the church. The church's ministry is multifaceted, just as any communion of people in relationships would be. Scripture describes this complex life of making disciples of Jesus in ways that help us to simplify the work and clearly see how we can avoid overcomplicating the life and ministry of the church. Scripture speaks of the church's ministry in two distinct but related ways, using two Greek words. What Scripture teaches us about the church's ministry will help us identify our own work as ministers in the church today.

The Bible uses an important term with reference to the church's ministry. The Greek word is *diakonos,* often translated deacon, servant, or minister. On occasion, the term refers to an office in the church. Deacons are chosen from the congregation to fulfill a unique function, typically associated with caring for members of the congregation and helping the church meet physical or financial needs (cf. Acts 6:1–6). First Timothy 3:8–13, for example, gives qualifications for those who will serve the church in the office of "deacon." Churches today use the term deacon almost exclusively with reference to the office.

However, the term *diakonos* is also used more broadly with reference to the church's ministry of service to one another. Jesus served his disciples (Mark 10:45). Martha served Jesus (John 12:2). The Christians in Macedonia served Paul (2 Cor 11:8). Churches took up offerings to serve those facing famine and shortage of food (Acts 11:29; 2 Cor 8:4). In Eph 4:11–12, teachers in the church "equip the saints for the work of ministry," which is the term *diakonos*, servant. Importantly, in 1 Cor 12:5, Paul instructs the church to remember that there are many different "services" or "ministries" in the church by which God's mission is fulfilled. Christians serve in many different ways in the church. For instance, when Paul was in prison, he spoke of those who ministered to him during that time (2 Tim 1:18).

Ministry also refers to the work of proclaiming the gospel. The work of the apostles is called the "ministry of the word" (Acts 6:4). Paul calls himself a minister of the Lord (1 Cor 3:5), of the new covenant (2 Cor 3:6), and of the church (Col 1:25). He describes his work of preaching the gospel to others as his "ministry of reconciliation" (2 Cor 5:18; Acts 20:24). The same is true of Timothy (1 Tim 4:6) and Epaphras (Col 1:7); they are ministers of God and of his church. First Peter 4:10–11 describes the church's ministry this way:

> Just as each one has received a gift, use it to *serve* others, as good stewards of the varied grace of God. If anyone speaks, let it be as one who speaks God's words; if anyone *serves*, let it be from the strength God provides, so that God may be glorified through Jesus Christ in everything. [emphasis added]

Every member of the church participates in the ministry of the church by ministering to one another in physical as well as spiritual ways. The church's ministry involves caring for those in need, helping those who hurt, and proclaiming the gospel of Jesus to people so they can conform their lives to it.

Who Are the Church's Ministers?

We have just seen that Scripture urges every Christian to *minister* to one another in the church. God gifts members for the purpose of caring for one another, helping one another, and discipling one another. There is not a unique class of church members or other Christians who solely do the work of ministry. With that being said, Scripture does identify several offices or positions within the church that do serve particular roles within the church's ministry. Those holding these offices have the responsibility to lead the members of the church in fulfilling the mission of the church. Those who occupy these offices are, for the sake of this volume, the disciple-makers who serve as the church's ministers.

Ephesians 4:11–12 becomes a crucial text for identifying the church's ministers. While the list of ministry positions in this passage may not be exhaustive, it does provide a starting place for what fulfilling the church's ministry looks like. In this passage are five (or perhaps four, see below) offices that Paul references: apostles, prophets, evangelists, pastors, and teachers, although the last two may refer to a single office.

An "apostle" generally is a messenger, someone who is "sent out" with a message to deliver. Apostles serve as representatives of the one who sent them. In Phil 2:25, Paul calls Epaphroditus an apostle, or messenger, because he was sent out as a representative of the church at Philippi. Second Corinthians 8:23 speaks of anonymous apostles of the church. Acts 14 tells us that Paul and Barnabas were apostles of the church because they were sent out as messengers and representatives of the church. Timothy is called an apostle of the church in 1 Thess 2:6, as are Junia and Andronicus in Rom 16:7. In each of these instances, the term apostle is used in the general sense of being "sent out" from the church.

There is also the usage of "apostle" with reference to the apostles of Jesus. This use of the term, and therefore the office it refers to, is different from the general usage seen above. Whereas there were many apostles of the church, there are only a select number—the Twelve plus Paul—who were apostles of Christ. These were the apostles who, along with the prophets, were the foundation of the church (Eph 2:20). The resurrected Christ had appeared to each of these men and commissioned them personally to deliver his message (Acts 1:21–25). The apostles received the gospel of Jesus directly from the risen Lord and delivered that to the believers who gathered to form churches. The message that the church preached and taught was received from the apostles, who had received it from Jesus (Acts 2:42). The writings of the New Testament contain this apostolic message. Only those to whom the risen Christ appeared could be considered apostles in this narrow sense. Ephesians 4:11 is perhaps using the term in the general sense, in which God gave to the church messengers who would represent the church in other locations, just as Epaphroditus had done in representing the Philippian church to Paul. Those sent out from the church to minister to others, perhaps like missionaries, help the church fulfill its mission of fulfilling the Great Commission.

A second role in the Ephesians passage is that of prophet. God has given those who speak to the people as gifts to the church "for their strengthening, encouragement, and consolation" (1 Cor 14:3). In contrast to someone who speaks in tongues, Paul says that the prophet "builds up the church" rather than building up himself (v. 4). God gifts the church with those who prophesy "so that everyone may learn and everyone may be encouraged" (v. 31). Clearly, prophets are those who proclaim the good news of Jesus to strengthen the faithful. Prophesying in the church began at Pentecost in the second chapter of Acts. Peter interprets the proclamation of the gospel of Jesus in Jerusalem as the fulfillment of a passage in the Old Testament book of Joel: "And it will be in the last days, says God, that I will pour out my Spirit on all people; then your sons and your daughters will prophesy" (Acts 2:17). While "prophecy" is often understood as "foretelling," as in promising some future event, Scripture most often uses the term with reference to "telling-forth," as in proclaiming God's truth. Peter interprets the proclaiming of the gospel to those gathered in Jerusalem "from all nations" as the fulfillment of Joel's message about the Spirit-empowered prophesying to come in the last day. Throughout the New Testament, those prophesying—or proclaiming the gospel—strengthened, encouraged, taught, and edified believers to help them grow in their relationship with Christ.

Paul speaks of a third gift of God to the churches in Eph 4:11, the role of evangelist, a term used only a handful of times in the Bible. Like apostle and prophet, when used of ministers within the church, "evangelist" refers to the role to which God calls men and women in service to the church and on behalf of the church. Timothy is told to "do the work of an evangelist" in fulfilling his ministry to the church (2 Tim 4:5). He does not hold a formal position of "evangelist" in the church but is called to fulfill that function as a minister. Philip is likewise called an evangelist because he preached the gospel to unbelievers that they might be converted (Acts 21:8). Within the church, God calls some to help the church fulfill its mission through gospel proclamation to the world, and not just to the church itself. Prophets, it would seem, speak the gospel within the church and evangelists speak the gospel outside of the church.

A fourth gift of God to the church in this passage is that of pastor. The Greek term refers to a shepherd, someone who cares for sheep. In the Bible, the term becomes a metaphor for those who minister to the people of God. Jesus himself is portrayed as the Good Shepherd in John 10:11–14, with his disciples being the sheep of his flock in Luke 12:32. When commissioning Peter before his ascension, Jesus told the apostle to "shepherd my sheep" (John 21:16). Peter then passes this same command on to elders in the church, telling them to "shepherd God's flock among you" (1 Pet 5:2).

The metaphor is a powerful one. There are those ministers in the church whom God calls specifically to a ministry of watching over the souls of men and women, guarding them from danger and leading them to safe pastures. Pastors instruct and correct in order to help the church make disciples by "teaching them to obey" everything Jesus has instructed. For this reason, it is possible that the last "gift" is inextricable from the fourth one. The final "office" or role can be read as pastor-teacher, rather than dividing the two roles from one another. In either case, the fact remains that teaching is a vital part of the church's ministry. In Acts 5:42, we read, "Every day in the temple, and in various homes, they continued teaching and proclaiming the good news that Jesus is the Messiah." The church cannot fulfill its mission without teaching the gospel. The apostle Paul was not only himself a teacher (Acts 20:20), but he also instructed the Colossian Christians to all teach one another (Col 3:16).

The Minister's Unique Role

In the end, the church's ministers are those members who answer the call of God to "equip the saints for the work of ministry, to build up the body of Christ" (Eph 4:12). As the entire congregation is called to share in the work of the gospel, the servant-leaders of the church are called to equip them for that work. A biblical model of this sort of ministry is found in the books of 1 and 2 Timothy. These books help shape a vision for ministry that is grounded in God's purpose for the church to make disciples of Jesus.

In 1 Timothy, Paul offers instructions for Christian living. People should remember the gospel, walk by faith, avoid false teaching, and develop a godly character. Christians should pray, obey their rulers, and pass along the faith to others in the church. Then Paul turns to Timothy and says, "If you point these things out to the brothers and sisters, you will be a good servant [minister] of Christ Jesus" (1 Tim 4:6). Faithful ministry entails helping others rightly follow

Jesus. But this type of ministry is built on the foundation of a life of Christian fidelity. Paul instructs, "Train yourself in godliness" (v. 7). To help others mature in Christ, the minister must first train themselves to mature in Christ.

Paul then turns his attention to three tasks that the faithful minister in the church must do. First, the minister is to "command and teach these things" (1 Tim 4:11). Every Christian is called to live *Christianly*. There are not two classes of believer, one class that is called to a high standard of obedience and another class that is not. All believers should strive to follow Jesus fully, without reserve or delay. But the minister has the unique task of teaching the church what to do and how to do it. Ministers are those tasked with instructing other disciples.

Second, in verse 12, Paul instructs Timothy to "set an example for the believers in speech, in conduct, in love, in faith, and in purity." Church ministry that follows the biblical pattern includes modeling the Christian life for the church. Christian ministers do not simply teach the faith, they must model the faith, serving as an example for church members. For example, if Christians are to learn how to love one another, then they must see this modeled for them. Ministers are those called to provide that example. Ministers must be able to say along with the apostle Paul, "Imitate me, as I also imitate Christ" (1 Cor 11:1).

Finally, the model of ministry Paul establishes for Timothy is to care for those members who are in need. The apostle tells Timothy, "Support widows who are genuinely in need" (1 Tim 5:3). The minister's role is not limited to teaching people what is true or even modeling for them authentic Christian living. While all members of the church are called to care for one another, how much more is the calling for the church's leaders to care for those in genuine need! Showing compassion is an essential part of the biblical model of Christian ministry. Ministers who fail to care for the "sheep" in their flock are destined for frustration and broken relationships. As we will see later (chapter 8), relationships are the vehicle by which the minister's teaching becomes transformative in the life of the church.

The model in 2 Timothy likewise begins with Paul's admonition, "Hold onto the pattern of sound teaching that you have heard from me" (2 Tim 1:13). Faithful ministry as a disciple-maker is always built on the foundation of being a mature disciple of Jesus. The minister must constantly be on guard against drifting from the gospel of Jesus. Walking with Jesus is a prerequisite to serving Jesus.

Second, Paul instructs Timothy to devote himself entirely to the work of the ministry, not becoming "entangled in the concerns of civilian life" (2 Tim 2:4). Soldiers, athletes, and farmers become metaphors for the life of the minister. Each of those figures is sold out unreservedly to the task at hand. Soldiers do whatever their commander expects, athletes compete for a prize to be won, and farmers work hard in order to reap the harvest. Ministers, similarly, serve Jesus because of the fruit of their labors: the progress of the gospel.

Third, the minister is to "correct, rebuke, and encourage with great patience and teaching" (2 Tim 4:2). Faithful ministers care for the people of God by correcting their sinful behavior, rebuking them when they offer false teaching in place of the gospel, and encouraging them in their walk with Jesus. Importantly, each of these tasks related to instruction are to be done "with great patience." The faithful minister is not a disciplinarian who punishes members of the church for falling short or being ignorant. Instead, the minister takes it upon himself to be patient with people, teaching them how to be faithful disciples.

The Unique Purpose of Christian Ministry

Jesus gave a unique mission to the church: make disciples. And every Christian is invited to participate in this mission as a follower of Jesus. But the Great Commission was issued to the church, the Body of Christ. Christians, who by their union with one another form the church, fulfill this mission in relationship to one another.

In order to "make disciples," the church identifies those within the body who are called to teach, lead, and encourage the body toward their common end. Every Christian is expected to share the gospel within their family and with their friends.[1] But sharing Jesus is not fulfilling the ministry. The ministry is uniquely tied to the church's common mission.

There may be missionaries, evangelists, denominational employees, seminary professors, etc., but even their calling to ministry is in association with the congregation, the gathered people of God. And while there are principles that can benefit everyone involved in the proclamation of the gospel, the main focus is on those who serve within the local church in fulfilling its ministry.

---

[1] See D. Scott Hildreth and Steven A. McKinion, *Sharing Jesus without Freaking Out*, 2nd ed. (Nashville: B&H Academic, 2020).

The Moral Requirements of Christian Ministry

In 1 Tim 4:16, the apostle Paul instructs the minister, "Pay close attention to your life and your teaching; persevere in these things, for in doing this you will save both yourself and your hearers." The immense pressure of paying close attention to "your life" in order to bring salvation to one's hearers can be overwhelming. Ministers have no problem acknowledging the significance of paying close attention to their teaching. Studying for messages to ensure fidelity to the gospel is never in question. While there may be an awareness of the necessity of proper teaching, rarely does that awareness lead to stress (though one might argue it should cause more angst than it sometimes does).

What makes "paying attention to your life" a challenge for the ministry is the unavoidable fact that the minister's own personal morality and Christian formation is inextricable for his or her calling. When a pastor is caught in adultery or some other immoral behavior, his vocation suffers irreparable harm (not to mention his family!). The job of being a pastor requires more than adherence to ethical standards, but never less. And those ethical standards are themselves part and parcel of the work of ministry.

Every profession has a code of ethics. Lawyers, doctors, nurses, and mechanics adhere to professional standards. But the doctor is not seeking to help her patient likewise learn and follow that code of behavior. A mechanic should not perform work that is unwarranted, or else he would act unethically. His own ethical behavior is vitally important. But the purpose of a mechanic's ethical behavior is the protection of his customer. The lawyer acts "professionally" for the benefit of his clients. The doctor follows a code of conduct to keep her patients safe. But a minister acts morally as a part of his effort to instruct others in how they should live.

Because faithful Christian living is a fundamental part of the ministry, every area of a minister's life comes under scrutiny. The pastor who is an excellent preacher but an immoral liar would disqualify himself from ministry. The Christian teacher who serves faithfully at church week after week, but is unkind, fails in performance of their duty.

My dad showed antipathy towards the church when I was a kid. I never understood why my mom had to take my younger brother and me to church each week (usually kicking and screaming in opposition), while my dad stayed home. He eventually returned to Christ and the church later in life. It was not until I was an adult that he explained his distrust of Christianity.

Dad became a Christian at Vacation Bible School at the local Baptist church. He parents did not really attend church, but he got involved with the youth group, serving in a variety of ways and growing in his faith. During college he was a music minister in a church (a story I had never heard growing up). The pastor from his home church, who had spent considerable time discipling him, ended up being removed from ministry due to unethical behavior. Having few other Christian influences in his life, my dad was devastated. Before long he left the ministry, left college, and left the church. For more than a decade he rejected church because of a pastor's failure.

Longevity in ministry requires ministers to be careful about areas of their own lives which might wreck the souls of those in their care. If a mechanic becomes an alcoholic, his customers don't stop getting their cars repaired. But if a minister fails to watch after his life, Christians may stop caring for their own spiritual lives.

The emphasis on the minister's care for his own moral living is not meant to be an added stressor. Instead, one significant indicator of eventual burnout in ministry is a growing distance between the pastor's life and his teaching. Sound teaching will take the pastor a long way in ministry. Very few people see "behind the curtain" into the pastor's life and home. A charismatic leader can mask fault lines in his character for a long time, decades even. A caring minister who "shows up" when people are hurting may actually be hiding deep and abiding questions about the ministry or unchristian attitudes towards people. People within a minister's church may not be able to see those fault lines. Perhaps they are unwilling to see them because of the benefit they seem to be getting.

Imagine someone who is a naturally caring and nurturing person. He or she truly loves Jesus and loves people. That person faithfully serves others, helping them to learn about Christ and grow in Christian maturity. Without constant attention to their own spiritual maturity, that person may begin to substitute care of others for consistency in spiritual formation. That minister may unwittingly adopt attitudes or behaviors that are inconsistent with the ministry in which they are engaged. A minister who is not maturing spiritually endangers both himself and those he is ministering to. The church suffers immense harm when the shepherd is exposed as a hypocrite. And the minister suffers from the rotting of his soul.

Failure to care for one's own soul while ministering to others leads to two possible outcomes. One, the pastor may come to question the mission and message. I had a pastor who was leaving the ministry ask me one time, "If I could pretend to be holy for so long, how can the message I was preaching each week help anyone else?" This minister burned out from ministry because his life did not reflect his teaching.

Second, the minister may become so weary with the explicit hypocrisy that he longs to abandon ministry just to get some help. I spoke with a former minister at a church I served who was caught in a serious moral failing. The moral indiscretions had been part of his life for almost three decades. He was a well-known and respected leader. He had found a way to conceal his immorality while being actively involved in ministry. Often he spoke to me and others about burnout. I thought he was tired *from* the ministry, but really he was tired *of* the ministry. When his sin was disclosed, he expressed relief. He was like the escaped prisoner who had grown weary of being on the run. Always looking over his shoulder, afraid he would be caught, caused anxiety and depression. He was "burned out" because he failed to watch his life with great care. Scores of people suffered when he was exposed and it did not need to come to that end. Faithful ministry requires faithful living. There is no substitute for sincere devotion to Jesus Christ as his disciple. No amount of giftedness or ingenuity in ministry will ever lead to genuine spiritual fruit.

With ministry there are unique pressures for those in that vocation that make burnout more likely, and more dangerous. For example, a doctor can become burned out from working 80-hour weeks. She can decide that family is more important that pursuing status. But if a physician is burned out, she can leave her job, or even her career, and pursue something else. However, participating in the ministry is not an "option" for those who assume that role. The church identifies those who have a call to ministry (see chapter 2). Participation in that vocation is different than any other vocation. It might be tempting to equate those vocations, but they are different. How?

"Ministry" is the church's gospel purpose. In order to fulfill the ministry, the church identifies those who will take on unique positions of teaching, leadership, and modeling to help the community of faith fulfill its purpose. These positions may have different titles (and functions) in different churches or different Christian traditions. They may be called pastors, elders, deacons, deaconesses, ministers, bishops, overseers, superintendents, directors, teachers, or any host of other possible titles. While each church, denomination, or tradition may view these positions differently (or use different names for the same position), what is important is the recognition that some in the church have a unique commission from the church to help the congregation become more effective (or effective at all) in fulfilling the congregation's mission.

In this volume, minister refers to anyone who (1) is recognized by the church as helping the congregation fulfill its mission and (2) self-identifies as someone who has responded to an inner and outer "call" to serve the church in a unique way, set apart and commissioned by the congregation for that purpose.

The ministry belongs to the church, not to the minister. The minister occupies some spot within the community to help the church fulfill its ministry. People are identified within the church to help the church. Ministers are not simply accomplishing their own work but are fulfilling their calling when they help the whole church. For this reason, there is something of an organization. The larger the community, the more extensive and expansive the organization. Take a church of ten people. A single person could easily occupy the role of teaching that congregation, leading them to remain faithful to the gospel, and helping form them into a ministering community. But a church of ten thousand people will look different. There will need to be an enormous organization to help that congregation fulfill its ministry. Even if there is a single main leader or teacher at the church, the work of the ministry requires a significant number of other people, each of whom are helping the church fulfill its mission. For our purposes, any and all of those self-identifying and identified by the church as ministers are participating in the "ministry" of the church.

The model for ministry that best reflects the pattern of the New Testament, and therefore creates the best environment for the minister to avoid burnout, is a *shared* ministry where everyone in the church participates in the church's purpose according to their spiritual giftedness (1 Corinthians 12). Churches where the ministers are the only ones *doing* ministry are not healthy for the church or the minister. Christians who never exercise their giftedness in helping fulfill the church's mission do not grow into spiritual maturity and miss the overwhelming blessing that comes from serving Jesus. Ministers who alone bear the burden of ministry become overworked and overwhelmed to the point of burnout. No one wins in that sort of ministry.

For ministers to fulfill their calling, as we saw previously in 1 and 2 Timothy, they must teach people to be disciples, model the disciple's life for people, and help the church care for one another. If the minister is a leader within the ministry rather than the sole doer of the ministry, everyone benefits, particularly those who are growing in Christ because of faithful ministry. The minister must learn to be a disciple-making leader, not just a disciple-maker. Becoming a leader in the ministry entails training others to share fully in the work of the church.

It is not enough to enlist people into the ministry. The servant-leader also must equip them for that work of ministry (Eph 4:12). The teaching ministry of the church is not just training in righteous living but is also training in fulfilling the church's purpose. Enlisting members in ministry and equipping members for ministry leads to empowering members to minister. Having been equipped to care for one another, the members of the church can confidently begin to live out the various "one another" commands of the New Testament:

- Love one another sincerely (1 Pet 1:22)
- Honor one another above yourselves (Rom 12:10)
- Live in harmony with one another (Rom 12:16)
- Instruct one another (Rom 15:14)
- Serve one another in love (Gal 5:13)
- Bear with one another in love (Eph 4:2)
- Submit to one another out of reverence to Christ (Eph 5:21)

- Forgive one another (Col 3:13)
- Speak to one another in psalms, hymns, and spiritual songs (Col 3:16)
- Live in peace with one another (1 Thess 5:13)
- Be kind to one another (1 Thess 5:15)
- Have fellowship with one another (1 John 1:7)

While there are many other examples of instruction to minister to "one another," these few examples highlight the call on every member of the church to care for each other and share in the ministry of making disciples. No one is excused from the call to participate in the church's ministry. Therefore, the church's servant-leaders are called to enlist, equip, and empower church members to fulfill their own calling.

Conclusion

Ministry is hard for a host of reasons. It can become a burden, though it is truly possible for it to be a blessing as well. We will tackle the unique challenges of ministry throughout this book so that you will be aware of the pitfalls that can turn a blessing into a burden, leading to burnout. Because your calling to ministry is to participate in the work of the Spirit of God by helping men and women come to know Christ and then fulfill their own mission as the church of God, you may fail to focus on the real purpose of your ministry. Failing to do so will lead to frustration and failure. Begin with the end in mind. You are called to serve the church by serving people who want to mature as followers of Jesus. And this biblical view of the church's ministry, and your part within it, serves as the foundation for a lifetime of faithful service to the church and through the church. With a proper understanding of the church's purpose as a solid foundation, you can begin to build a ministry of serving Jesus without burning out.

{ CHAPTER 2 }

The Sustaining Power of Your Call

Therefore, since we have this ministry because
we were shown mercy, we do not give up.
Instead, we have renounced secret and shameful
things, not acting deceitfully or distorting
the word of God, but commending ourselves
before God to everyone's conscience by an
open display of the truth. But if our gospel is
veiled, it is veiled to those who are perishing. In
their case, the god of this age has blinded the
minds of the unbelievers to keep them from
seeing the light of the gospel of the glory of
Christ, who is the image of God. For we are not
proclaiming ourselves but Jesus Christ as Lord,
and ourselves as your servants for Jesus's sake.

—2 Cor 4:1–5

Principle: You did not choose the job; the job chose you.

Introduction

A successful missionary described her first months on the field:

> It was so hard. Nothing made sense. I couldn't talk or understand. My family seemed to be suffering. I see now that I was in full-blown culture shock. One day, a friend from the United States called to check on me. We talked about her life and things back at home, everything I was missing. Not long into the conversation, she started to pile on the praise. She talked about how proud she was of me and how inspiring my commitment was to her. She was a good friend, so I felt I could be honest, so I said, "Please stop that right now. I don't even like it here. The food is bad, the people are not friendly, my kids are sick, and I'm usually scared. *If not for my firm conviction that God called me here, I would be on the next airplane."*

A student in a seminary told the story of sitting in the back of a taxi in India. He was at the end of a mission trip, training local pastors and staying in harsh conditions—sleeping and eating in less-than-ideal conditions.

The route back to the hospital took him through a wealthy community, directly in front of an opulent hotel. "Tears started rolling down my face before I knew what was happening. You see, a couple of years before, I had been working for an international business and stayed in the penthouse suite of this same hotel. I spent the week partying, spending loads of money, and making business deals.

But in that moment, I sensed God reminding me of the importance of my new work building his kingdom. *I knew God was calling me to serve him by taking the gospel to those who had never heard.*"

These ministry leaders learned the power of clinging to God's call. It became a source of life change and endurance. It gave them purpose and hope in moments of crisis. Christian ministry is challenging. We are often misunderstood and maligned, and the work can feel meaningless. These experiences are often a recipe for burnout. This chapter will explore the meaning and reality of God's call to ministry. We will also show how revisiting and remembering that God has called us to ministry can sustain us in the work.

Oswald Chambers observed that God's call to ministry is not easy to describe, "the sudden awareness of this incalculable, supernatural, surprising call that has taken hold of your life."[1] The minister often experiences this sense that God says, "I have chosen you." Christian ministry is not like any other job. While there was certainly a day you decided to pursue this work, you did not choose it. Indeed, God chose you for his service. God did not choose you because of your sanctification, skill, or pedigree. As Paul reminded Timothy, God's call to ministry is for his glory, that "Christ Jesus might demonstrate his extraordinary patience as an example to those who would believe in him for eternal life" (1 Tim 1:16). Consider these words from Henry Blackaby, "One does not choose ministry! A pastor is chosen. He is

---

[1] Oswald Chambers, *My Utmost for His Highest,* updated ed. (Grand Rapids: Discovery House, 2017).

chosen by God for God's purposes, in God's time and place, and serves Him in God's ways."[2] God doesn't call men and women to ministry based on worth or ability; his call makes us worthy and qualifies us for the task.

The Call of God

Most Bible teachers identify at least two types of callings. First, the universal call that belongs to every believer. This call begins with God's call to salvation—his invitation to leave the darkness and come into the light.

- "God is faithful; you were called by him into fellowship with his Son, Jesus Christ our Lord" (1 Cor 1:9).
- "As you know, like a father with his own children, we encouraged, comforted, and implored each one of you to walk worthy of God, who calls you into his own kingdom and glory" (1 Thess 2:11–12).
- "The God of all grace, who called you to his eternal glory in Christ, will himself restore, establish, strengthen, and support you after you have suffered a little while. To him be dominion forever. Amen" (1 Pet 5:10–11).

Left to ourselves, no one seeks God. Because we were spiritually dead, we focused our energies on self-preservation and self-promotion. However, the Bible tells us that God, in his great grace, invited us to himself to

[2] Henry T. Blackaby, Henry Brandt, and Kerry L. Skinner, *The Power of the Call* (Nashville: Broadman & Holman, 1997), 21.

receive forgiveness of sin and to live in a dynamic relationship with our creator.

This call is universal because no one is excluded. After his resurrection, Jesus told his disciples that God's plan from the beginning has been for the nations to repent and receive forgiveness from sin (Luke 24:47). This call includes people from every tribe, people, and language (Rev 7:9). It is God's will that everyone be saved and come to the knowledge of the truth (1 Tim 2:4).

Scott Pace has observed that God's universal call is not limited to salvation. This calling also includes a general call to service. As Gal 5:13 says, "For you were called to be free, brothers and sisters; only don't use this freedom as an opportunity for the flesh, but serve one another through love." No Christian is too important to serve others. Jesus told us that he did not come to be served but to serve (Mark 10:45). If our Lord took up the mantle of service, we should not anticipate a different life.[3]

Along with the call to serve, each Christian also receives a universal call to surrender. We read about this call in Paul's words in Eph 4:1, "Therefore I, the prisoner in the Lord, urge you to walk worthy of the calling you have received." Our response to God's call to salvation includes giving up rights to our lives. We recognize that we are his, bought with the precious blood of Jesus. Because of this, every Christian has a calling that demands submission to whatever he places before us.

---

[3] R. Scott Pace, *Answering God's Call: Finding, Following, and Fulfilling God's Will for Your Life* (Nashville: B&H Academic, 2020).

In addition to this universal calling, the Bible also contains examples of a more specific, individual calling. Scott Pace notes that this call embraces the reality that "The Lord has chosen *you* to serve him in a particular way, at a specific place and time, with a unique combination of talents and gifts, for his strategic purposes."[4] Oswald Chambers says about this special ministry calling, "[it] has nothing to do with salvation and sanctification. You are not called to preach the gospel because you are sanctified; the call to preach the gospel is infinitely different."[5]

Each of us experiences this call in different ways. But, at the very least, it comes with a keen awareness that something in our world is not what it should be, and we can not be content until we address it. Here is a list of the types of concerns that can lead to a call to ministry:

- A preacher is frustrated by the lack of biblical knowledge and the trouble this ignorance enables.
- A seminary or college professor is compelled by a concern for the theological development of Christian leaders, missionaries, and local church ministers.
- A missionary is distressed by the countless millions with little or no access to the gospel.
- A worship leader is overwhelmed by the glory of God and senses a desire to help God's people lift Him up.
- A children's or student minister is driven to help families and younger boys and girls grow in Christ, hoping the next generation will not be lost.

---

[4] Pace, *Answering God's Call*, 4.

[5] Chambers, *My Utmost for His Highest.*

- A Christian counselor sees the world's brokenness and is driven by the desire to apply biblical principles to these areas of pain.

It is impossible to fully describe the inner passion because it is an individual experience. But this sense of need, combined with an opportunity for service and some affirmation of gifting, caused each of us to commit our lives to Christian ministry. We "surrendered" to vocational ministry in response to God's initiative—choosing us for himself.

The Biblical Vision for Ministry

Perhaps one of the most vivid descriptions of Christian ministry comes in Paul's second letter to the Corinthian church. Apparently, his previous letter had caused some hurt and division within the community. Then, in the middle of this interpersonal conflict, rival ministers arrived and took advantage of the dissension and frustration with Paul to bolster their own standing. David Garland writes, "The result: some members continue as avid supporters of Paul, some waver, and some comprise a determined element of resistance . . . *Anyone who has held a position of leadership in a church can probably identify with this scenario.*"[6]

In the face of this crisis, Paul pens a profoundly personal reflection on Christian ministry. As he reflects on his vocation, he also highlights the importance of the call to

---

[6] David E. Garland, *2 Corinthians*, New American Commentary, vol. 29 (Nashville: Broadman & Holman, 1999), 26, emphasis added.

ministry. As we meditate on this passage, the Scriptures can serve as a healing salve for our weary souls and a reminder of the significance of this work we do.

> But thanks be to God, who always leads us in Christ's triumphal procession and through us spreads the aroma of the knowledge of him in every place. For to God, we are the fragrance of Christ among those who are being saved and among those who are perishing. To some we are an aroma of death leading to death, but to others, an aroma of life leading to life. Who is adequate for these things? For we do not market the word of God for profit like so many. On the contrary, we speak with sincerity in Christ, as from God and before God. (2 Cor 2:14–17)

We Serve as Those Conquered by God's Goodness

In the face of criticism from those outside and, perhaps most painfully, those inside the church, Paul reflects on an unusual image of ministry. In v. 14, he remembers that his life and ministry are under the control and at the command of a conquering king.

The phrase "who always leads us in Christ's triumphal procession" has been understood by some as a cry of victory. The idea is that Paul finds hope by clinging to the thought that, even in the face of criticism, he is in God's army. He marches in the victory parade with the resurrected Jesus. However, this interpretation does not fit with Paul's chosen wording. Rather than choosing a word that might be understood as Paul including himself in the victory march, the image invoked here is that his role is of a captured and conquered slave.

Thriambeuomai (Paul's word translated here "triumphal procession") was used to describe the humiliating parade that occurred when a victorious general showed off the spoils of his victory. In this imagery, Paul envisions himself—and the rest of us who serve in Christian ministry—as those having been conquered by God. Garland has noted that Paul "does not represent himself as a garlanded, victorious general nor as a foot soldier in God's army who shares in the glory of Christ's triumph. Quite the opposite; he portrayed himself as a conquered prisoner on display. He was previously God's enemy but is now defeated, being led to death in a display that reveals the majesty and power of God and effectively proclaimed the Gospel."[7]

In the face of opposition and exhausting circumstances, one of Paul's foundational presuppositions about his life and ministry was that, at one time, he was God's enemy, but God, in his rich goodness, conquered his rebellious heart. Rather than serving God with his head held high, proud to play an integral part on the winning team, Paul's enduring strength comes from the thought that, left to his own choices, he would have willingly remained part of the opposing army. Now, by God's grace, he has been called into service—his life and ministry reflect God's grace and the glory of the redemptive promise in the gospel.

This discussion brings to memory the old-school phrase used by preachers and missionaries to describe their lives. The step of saying "yes" to God's call is often referred to as

---

[7] Garland, *2 Corinthians*, 141.

"surrendering." This isn't a bad image as we remember that when God selected us for his service, he tapped a former enemy as an ambassador.

We can endure hardships, humiliations, and hostilities because we know that our lives are under the command of a good God who leads us in his victory parade. Paul communicated the same idea in his first letter to Timothy (who seemed to have been facing a difficult time in ministry).

> I give thanks to Christ Jesus our Lord who has strengthened me, because he considered me faithful, appointing me to the ministry—even though I was formerly a blasphemer, a persecutor, and an arrogant man. But I received mercy because I acted out of ignorance in unbelief, and the grace of our Lord overflowed, along with the faith and love that are in Christ Jesus. This saying is trustworthy and deserving of full acceptance: "Christ Jesus came into the world to save sinners"—and I am the worst of them. But I received mercy for this reason, so that in me, the worst of them, Christ Jesus might demonstrate his extraordinary patience as an example to those who would believe in him for eternal life. Now to the King eternal, immortal, invisible, the only God, be honor and glory forever and ever. Amen. (1 Tim 1:12–17)

The reformer Martin Luther observed, "God creates out of nothing. Therefore, until a man is nothing, God cannot make anything out of him." Burnout happens when we get stuck in the frustrations and hardships in ministry without remembering our purpose. If we confuse earthly success with God's plan for our lives, it is easy to tap out or walk away.

We Serve as a Channel for the Knowledge of God

Having established that our involvement in Christian ministry is in response to God's winning our rebellious hearts to himself, Paul then shifts metaphors from servants to a savory aroma. Calvin uses this metaphor to refer to ministry as "perfuming the world with the health-giving odour of his grace."[8]

> . . . through us spreads the aroma of the knowledge of him in every place. For to God we are the fragrance of Christ among those who are being saved and among those who are perishing. (2 Cor 2:14–15)

New Testament scholars debate the source of this fragrance. Is it intended to refer to a sweet-smelling perfume, or does it point to the aroma created through sacrifice? There is support for each of these positions, but for our purposes, it is enough to realize Paul's point is that God uses each of us as the channel for spreading the fragrance of his gospel into a world that is overwhelmed with the stench of decay.

Consider for a moment how boundless a smell is! Who hasn't experienced the encroaching funk of a dirty diaper? I know some men pretend they don't smell it, but

---

[8] John Calvin, *Commentaries on the Epistles of Paul the Apostle to the Corinthians* (Bellingham, WA: Logos Bible Software, 2010), 158.

they do. On the other hand, when I visit my in-laws, I never set an alarm clock. The aroma of coffee and bacon floats out of the kitchen, up the stairs, and under the door. The boundless smell of a southern breakfast welcomes me to a new day.

We serve on location as a dispensary for the knowledge of him. Longing for a different location or a more straightforward ministry assignment is tempting. But we should remember that God has placed us in specific ministry locations to perfume the knowledge of the gospel. Frankly, with this understanding of ministry, we should anticipate difficulties. After all, think about what causes a fragrance to spread:

- Squeezing
- Heating up
- Pouring out
- Spreading thin

If we pause for a few minutes, it isn't difficult to imagine each of these words describing a season or aspect of ministry. On the other hand, one thought that does not serve as a source of fragrance is *peacefully bottled up.* None of us longs for life in a pressure cooker, but perhaps we can find hope in the realization that God has not abandoned us. Instead, he is using these events of our lives as the channel for knowledge of the good news.

The startling reality is that this good news is received differently. Paul notes, "To some [it is] an aroma of death . . . to others, an aroma of life" (2 Cor 2:16). Church father, John Chrysostom wrote of this verse:

> Soothing ointment is said to suffocate pigs. Light is blinding to the weak. It is in the nature of good things not only to correct what is close to them but also to destroy the opposite, and in this way their power is displayed. For so both fire, not only when it giveth light and when it purifieth gold, but even when it consumeth thorns, doth very greatly display its proper power, and so show itself to be fire.[9]

Our ministry—meaning our professional work and personal life—is a means to portraying the gospel to everyone who observes our life. This truth comforts, corrects, challenges, and encourages others in their own relationship with Jesus Christ. How we portray the Christian life can lead people to a deeper walk with Jesus or repel them from his call on their lives. Many hate what they do not understand, and in our day of online anger and social media criticism, the stench of death can become overwhelming.

The conviction that Christian ministers serve as the platform for the reality of the gospel leads Paul to the firm conviction that ministry is a life, not a job. As such, we must pursue it with "sincerity." This word carries the idea of being clear of impure motives. This is why we can say that ministry is unlike any other job. The very nature of the work is that it is not simply a task (or tasks) to be done. It is also a life to be lived.

---

[9] John Chrysostom, *Homilies on the Epistles of Paul to the Corinthians*, 5:3, in *1–2 Corinthians*, ed. Gerald Bray, Ancient Christian Commentary on Scripture, New Testament, vol. 7 (Downers Grove: InterVarsity, 1999), 211.

Beating Burnout

Even though we read the Bible, and it seems some men and women just "show up" in ministry, the consistent narrative shows God calls people to serve him.

- In Genesis 12, God called Abraham to leave his home and join God's plan for establishing a great nation from which the peoples of the earth would be blessed.
- In Exodus 3, God called Moses to proclaim his message to Pharaoh and lead the people to freedom.
- In Judges 6, God called Gideon to rescue the people from captivity and to serve as a righteous judge.
- In Isaiah 6, God called Isaiah to be his prophet, carrying his message to people who needed to hear the truth but who would reject it.
- In the Gospels, we read several encounters of Jesus calling ordinary men to join him and serve roles that would eventually become the foundation and pillars of the faith.
- In Acts, we read about the dramatic account of Jesus calling Saul from a murderous rampage to be the apostle to the unreached Gentiles.

Each of these stories includes dramatic encounters with God; however, it is a mistake to think these extremes are the only means of calling. Consider Paul's missionary team: Timothy, Titus, Silas, Epaphroditus, and others. These ministers seem to have experienced God's call through the guidance of other Christians or less dramatic circumstances. God's call comes in a variety of forms, dramatic or basic.

The theme of this chapter is that we did not choose this ministry; God chose us. This calling should not be reduced to an individual, mystical experience. It grows from the realization of God's rich mercy toward us and a growing awareness that something in the world is amiss. Most who discuss the significance of ministry calling highlight three areas of confirmation. As we encounter frustration in ministry, it may be helpful to revisit these.

First, the call to ministry includes an *internal* conviction. It may be a growing awareness of a need and the thought that "someone ought to do something." Perhaps it is the realization that millions have no hope or that the church is languishing in our culture for want of sound biblical teaching. Our eyes are opened, and once we have "seen" the need, we cannot "unsee" it. Bible study, sermons, songs, and prayer deepen our passions. The Holy Spirit uses these spiritual tools to fire our imaginations for what could be or, better, what should be.

At some point, we settle on the reality that "I" am the someone who needs to do something. Usually, this step isn't embraced with uber-confidence or pride but with a humble admission: "God, here I am. If you can use me, send me."

Second, this internal experience is always accompanied by *external* affirmation. We received validation through the counsel of a pastor, trusted friend, or spiritual mentor. Someone agreed they had observed God's work in our lives. They pointed out specific gifts and personality traits as beneficial for ministry. Let's not downplay this moment. Before we knew we needed someone's help, God placed these trusted individuals in our lives and prompted them to observe the traits we needed to validate. This further confirms that we didn't choose this work; God chose us.

Along with the external validation from trusted individuals, the call to ministry is confirmed by the church. This process is undoubtedly different for each person, but at some point, the private conversations and prayers became public. We preached our first sermon, taught a Bible study, or stepped into a leadership role. Maybe you volunteered, but more likely, someone asked you to do it. Then, as a result of this experience, the church affirmed our calling.

I [Scott] remember talking with my pastor about sensing a call to preach. After listening for several minutes, he said, "Well, if God called you to preach, then we need to get you on the calendar and see what happens."

To be honest, when I made an appointment with him to talk about a call to preach, I didn't think I was called to preach *now*. I didn't volunteer for the sermon. However, my pastor knew my internal call required external validation before it could mature into a vocational aspiration.

The ministry opportunity provides the opening for other Christians to affirm God's work in our lives. They point out how God used our message in their lives or that our leadership provided a platform for success. These comments can be understood as a validation of God's handiwork.

Finally, God's call is confirmed through ministry opportunities that he provides. Do you have a ministry position, a pulpit to preach in, a people group to reach, a role to fulfill? We should never believe that these opportunities are coincidental. The Lord of the universe worked in our hearts through his people and then orchestrated circumstances for us to obey his call. Sure, you may be where you are because of a good word from a friend or mentor. Maybe you applied for a job, or someone called to see if you'd be interested in a change. But you'd be mistaken to assume God was absent from this process. Remember, you didn't choose this ministry; it chose you.

Okay, but How Does This Help?

This journey down memory lane has been more than a reflection on the "good ole days." We hope that revisiting your journey into ministry and the affirmation of God's call on your life will give you support and help you endure, even if you feel like you are at the very end of your rope.

1. Perspective in the Grind

According to Elizabeth Saunders, writing in the *Harvard Business Review,* burnout happens when we feel overloaded and out of balance. It is the overwhelming feeling of being required to do more than reasonably possible.[10] It is endless toil and a to-do list that extends beyond anyone's ability to finish it. This is Christian ministry. As such, if we cannot approach it with a healthy perspective, we will burn out.

Burnout is largely the result of unhealthy rhythms in life rather than unbalanced calendars. Avoiding burnout is not simply balancing all of life's responsibilities but learning to align our lives with God's call. Remember the call of God gives us freedom to decline invitations and navigate

---

[10] Elizabeth Grace Saunders, "6 Causes of Burnout and How to Avoid Them," *Harvard Business Review,* July 5, 2019, https://hbr.org/2019/07/6-causes-of-burnout-and-how-to-avoid-them.

unrealistic expectations. We learn to say no to good things in order to conform our lives to the best of God's purposes for us. We also discover that God is at work in the circumstances of life that may appear out of control. Busyness is not the root cause of burnout, purposelessness is. We can easily become frustrated in ministry when we no longer sense a divine purpose to our work. Remembering that we minister out of a sense of call, rather than a sense of duty, gives purpose to all we do.

2. Reason for Purity

Remembering that God has called us to a ministry and placed us among a people does more than provide perspective and the ability to say "no" to specific invitations. Perhaps more importantly, reflecting on God's call to ministry can also empower us to say "no" to temptations that would disqualify us and make it impossible to fulfill God's ministry.

The purpose of this book is to provide tools for finishing ministry well. It is true that many fail to finish well because of exhaustion and burnout. However, many other men and women don't finish well because of sinful or inappropriate behavior. This may be sexual sin, interpersonal conflict, pride, love of money, or the pursuit of power. The list is endless, but the path is the same: we take our eyes off God's assignment and forget that he chose the task for us.

We need to remember that ministry is not like other vocations. Consider Paul's warning to Timothy: "Pay close attention to your life and your teaching; persevere in these things, for in doing this you will save both yourself and your hearers" (1 Tim 4:16). It is tempting to assume that success in ministry rests on our ability to perform well or teach accurately. And, while it is true that we should strive for excellence in all we do, Paul reminded his pastoral protege—and us by extension—that discharging the full responsibility of ministry also includes watching our lives. Commenting on this passage, Thomas Lea reminds us, "The stumbles and fumbles of a wandering spiritual leader will infect a congregation with a variety of spiritual sicknesses."[11]

The gospel transforms the whole life. Sound belief, perseverance, and lifelong growth are the goal. Ministry is different because our lives, as well as the ministry activities we perform, are intertwined. Buying insurance from someone who is unfaithful to their spouse does not affect the policy. We vote for politicians with character flaws, and we even take medical advice from a physician who is overweight or smokes. But ministry is different. Robert Murray M'Cheyne, the Scottish pastor, is rumored to have said, "My people's greatest need is my personal holiness." Remembering this gives us the motivation to say "no." Since we didn't choose this ministry but pursued it because of God's call on our lives, we are not free simply to choose actions or activities because of our own interests. This is not our ministry to throw away or destroy.

3. Support in the Overwhelming Moments

Jesus's final words to his disciples provide us with encouraging support for the moments of ministry that threaten to

---

[11] Thomas D. Lea and Hayne P. Griffin Jr., *1, 2 Timothy and Titus,* New American Commentary, vol. 34 (Nashville: B&H, 1992), 141.

overwhelm us. In the Great Commission (Matt 28:18–20), Jesus gives his disciples a seemingly impossible assignment. They were charged with making disciples of every people group on the planet. In a time without airplanes, trains, or automobiles and when their persecution was increasing, Jesus seemed to double down on their ministry assignment.

The struggle is further complicated by the emotional state of these men when they received this commission—"When they saw him, they worshiped, but some doubted" (Matt 28:17). These men were not in a healthy emotional or spiritual state. Nerves were fried, faith shattered, and their hopes dashed. It is not difficult to imagine they felt a little foolish and abandoned. Then, Jesus gave them the weighty task of global discipleship.

The support Jesus offered was not a superpower or skill set. On the contrary, the success of their ministry was founded on the promise of Jesus's omnipresence—"And remember, I am with you always, to the end of the age" (Matt 28:20). Perhaps the most significant promise given anywhere in the Bible is the Lord's promise to be with us.

- When Abraham faced an unknown journey, God promised to be with him to show him the promised land (Genesis 12).
- When Moses struggled with insecurity in his call to proclaim his word to the mighty Pharaoh, God didn't comfort him with talent, but a promise, "I will certainly be with you . . ." (Exod 3:12).

- Joshua was called to follow a popular and influential leader, and God calmed his nerves with the promise, "I will be with you, just as I was with Moses. I will not leave you or abandon you" (Josh 1:5).
- David knew the calming experience of God's presence when he was in the dark valley—"I fear no danger, for you are with me" (Ps 23:4).
- When Jeremiah felt the pressure of his calling and was convinced he couldn't perform, God encouraged him by saying, "Do not be afraid of anyone, for I will be with you" (Jer 1:8).
- God was with Daniel in the lions' den and was with Shadrach, Meshach, and Abednego in the fire.
- The prophet Isaiah and the apostle Matthew remind us that our salvation arrived in Jesus—Immanuel, God with us.
- As Jesus sends his followers on his mission, he gives us the same promise: "I am with you always, to the end of the age" (Matt 28:20).

Our call to ministry is accompanied by the promise of God's presence. The ministry is his. He chose us for the task. Ministry can be lonely. We often feel isolated by the work and by the burdens that we are unable to offload. It is foolish to deny the reality of this pressure. However, the risen Christ, through the presence of his Spirit, is with us in the ministry. He has quite literally called us to join him, to labor alongside him, and to work with his strength. Our call to ministry rests on the most significant promise in the Bible, "I am with you."

4. A Reason to Persevere

Remembering God's call also serves as an anchor when the ministry gets stormy. It motivates us to endure when it is easier to quit. Reflecting on our calling also reminds us that God is good and he deserves the glory.

Charles Spurgeon is rumored to have said, "If God calls you to preach, do not stoop to become the King of England." Whether it was Spurgeon or someone else who said this, the truth remains. God's call supplies direction, shapes decisions, and helps us know when to accept or reject opportunities. Remembering God's call also serves as the reason to keep serving and sticking to the task before us.

The painful truth is that God's call is not something that makes all of life more manageable. It presents a genuine burden. The burden we are thinking about is not what Jeremiah expresses when he cries about God's message being like a fire in his bones (Jer 20:9). There is no doubt that this fire exists in all of us. As we noted earlier, this passion, along with the awareness of the need, is what God used to draw us. This passion is a weight we carry daily. However, the burden we are thinking about here is the daily knowledge that the God of the universe has enlisted you personally into his service. You heard this call and said, "Yes." At this point, we encounter the weight of obedience. It's a joy, but it is also a heavy responsibility.

Paul reminded Timothy of this burden when he wrote, "No one serving as a soldier gets entangled in the concerns of civilian life; he seeks to please the commanding officer. Also, if anyone competes as an athlete, he is not crowned unless he competes according to the rules. The hardworking farmer ought to be the first to get a share of the crops. Consider what I say, for the Lord will give you understanding in everything" (2 Tim 2:4–7).

As we strive to present everyone as perfect in Christ Jesus (see Ephesians 4), Christian ministry will be filled with pain and frustration as we pursue this call in a broken world. Ministry exposes the gravity of sin and the pain it causes. Perhaps the most painful reality is the fact that we are not only ministering to broken people in a broken world but that we ourselves are broken. This painful realization often causes us to throw in the towel and let someone else fight. But then the reality settles in: God called us here. We cannot just quit and walk away.

The Measurement of Ministry Success

Eugene Peterson reminds us that we should not measure obedience by a single act or decision: "If we define the nature of our lives by the mistakes of the moment or the defeat of the hour or the boredom of the day, we will define it wrongly."[12] Instead, he reminds us that the Christian life, and especially pastoral ministry, is a long obedience in the same direction. His challenge is that we evaluate our lives (and, by extension, our ministries) through a more robust lens—we connect the past, present, and promised future into what he calls an "organic unity."

---

[12] Eugene H. Peterson, *A Long Obedience in the Same Direction: Discipleship in an Instant Society*, 20th anniversary ed. (Downers Grove: InterVarsity, 2000), 169–70.

Remembering the call of God does not lighten the load or make each day of ministry blissful. However, it should serve as a healthy framework for the work as you remember this is not a task you chose; you were chosen for it. We cannot walk away or throw it away. It is wrong to judge success, failure, productivity, or time wasted by the events of a single experience or day. We persevere because we remember that God himself has placed us on this path with him. Because God is always working around us, we can confidently persevere in ministry, regardless of what the present circumstances might insinuate about our fruitfulness, because we are joining God in his ministry rather than seeking to do ministry on his behalf.

{ CHAPTER 3 }

Being God's Servant Where You Are, as You Are

But Moses replied to the Lord, "Please, Lord, I have never been eloquent—either in the past or recently or since you have been speaking to your servant—because my mouth and my tongue are sluggish." The Lord said to him, "Who placed a mouth on humans? Who makes a person mute or deaf, seeing or blind? Is it not I, the Lord? Now go! I will help you speak and I will teach you what to say." Moses said, "Please, Lord, send someone else."

—Exodus 4:10–13

Principle: You are the perfect person for your ministry.

Introduction

The attitude that you are not the right person for your given ministry may sow the seeds for burn out more than any other. Authenticity in ministry means serving in a way that is true to your identity in Jesus Christ and is consistent with your abilities, experiences, and the context in which you minister. Conversely, inauthenticity in ministry means pretending to be someone you are not. This may be emulating your hero in ministry to appear more intelligent, articulate, or sophisticated. Failing to live up to the image someone else holds makes you a phony. Whether in attitude or action, being fake in ministry harms the soul of the minister by causing him to question whether he belongs. You must understand your own identity in Christ and your subsequent identity as the minister God intends for you to be in order to have freedom to serve Jesus without the constant pressure to pretend to be someone you are not.

The origin of the term "sincere" captures the significance of authenticity in ministry. The term comes from the Latin words *sin* and *cere*. The word *sin* means "without," and the word *cere* means "wax." In the ancient world, items crafted from stone would often have cracks. Artisans would fill the cracks with wax to make them appear to be without blemish. Works which were "without wax" were those which did not purport to be something they were not. To be sincere means to be genuine or authentic. The minister does not have the luxury of covering up blemishes or filling in the cracks with wax that will melt away in the heat exposing the underlying flaws. If you fall into the trap of pretending in ministry, you will always be living in a double-minded way, acting with duplicity and dishonesty. We have known far too many ministers who burn out because of the weight of duplicitous living. The Bible reminds us, "Be sure your sin will catch up with you" (Num 32:23).

Authenticity is vitally important for relationships which form the bridge to ministry. What are the characteristics of authenticity? First is a sincere commitment to the gospel itself. Ministers often drift from a deep and abiding faith to one which only half-heartedly acknowledges the need people have for the gospel. Moreover, ministers might forget their own need for the presence and power of the Spirit in their ministry. Either not acknowledging the seriousness of the gospel or refusing to submit to the all-encompassing nature of the gospel to life, a minister can end up serving in his own strength or without confidence in God's Spirit to work in the lives of other people. Additionally, ministers may begin to doubt the message they are called to deliver. Doubts about the truthfulness of the Bible or the message of the Bible may occur. Numerous accounts of pastors who "deconvert" include a period of continued participation in ministry even after coming to reject the claims of Christ. Ministers who are on staff at a church may be afraid of losing income. Those who minister as volunteers may not want to let people down. The road to burnout, abandoning the church, and, for some, abandoning the faith often begins with service in ministry that is inauthentic and insincere.

Authenticity begins with a growing maturity about the claims of the gospel. This is one reason why Paul says to Timothy, not to lay hands on a novice. New believers are often the first to volunteer for ministry assignments in the church. Their newfound trust in Jesus revolutionizes their lives and they are eager to serve him. Besides temptation to sin, ministers who are young in the faith also face temptation to pride in ministry. It is wiser, it appears, to give believers time to become strong in their faith before subjecting them to the rigors of ministry.

Young ministers are looking to both discover who God made them to be and to develop into the minister their church needs them to be. Authenticity means giving attention to both discovery and development. Many ministers learn by imitation. We listen to other preachers, imitating their mannerisms, copying their outlines, and learning to turn a phrase in similar manner. There is nothing wrong with imitation in learning. But when imitation conceals the true personality or makeup of the minister, then growing into maturity stops. I recently heard about a calf who was rejected by his mother. The calf was nurtured by the farmer's dogs. The calf could mimic many of the canine behaviors, but never actually became a dog. More importantly, the calf was not maturing into the best representation of a cow! Ministers who never develop their own way of ministering, merely mimicking others, face a day of reckoning when they wake up and discover they are neither a good dog nor a good cow. A writer can learn a great deal about writing by imitating her favorite author, but eventually the writer must discover her own voice. Authentic ministers discover who *they* are.

A second characteristic of authentic ministry is telling the truth about your own ministry. In the social media generation, there is immense pressure to "appear" a certain way in order to compete with other pastors or churches. There is even the temptation to compete with other people in your own church. Pride is an enormous temptation in ministry because some ministries are more visible than others. Paul addresses this in 1 Cor 12:23–25 by reminding us that in the church's ministry both "honorable" and "dishonorable" ministries are deserving of recognition. Why are there no ministries in the church that are more valuable or honorable than others? Because there is only one Spirit by whom they function. Serving Jesus without burning out requires us to see our own ministry as one part of God's design to accomplish his purposes.

Another important characteristic of authentic ministry is becoming comfortable with your own identity in Christ. This characteristic is the most important, both for faithfulness in ministry and, for the purposes of this book, longevity in ministry. Avoiding burnout requires coming to grips with your own limitations. Plus, you must come to see your giftedness as the provision of the Spirit "for the common good," not the good of your reputation (1 Cor 12:7). Being a Christian is the foundation for ministry, not being a *gifted* Christian. In Christ, you already have the Spirit as the gift. Learning to walk in the Spirit and minister in the power of the Spirit is a far better guard against burnout than developing your skills at "leading people."

Ministry is a noble calling. Pastors have made a commitment to shepherding, guiding, and nurturing a community of believers. It is important to resist the urge to measure your own ministry against the perceived achievements of other ministers or churches. God has called you to lead your present church, not another church. Learning to serve Jesus faithfully where you are and how you are can help mitigate the sense of inadequacy that the curse of comparison causes.

Throughout this chapter you will be challenged to reflect on God's purpose in creating human beings, redeeming human beings in Christ, and reconciling human beings to himself. After all, the essence of the gospel is God's purpose to love humanity and create a people who dwell forever in the place he makes for them. The Bible reminds us that, "If anyone is in Christ, he is a new creation; the old has passed away, and see, the new has come!" (2 Cor 5:17). A lifetime of faithful ministry requires regular reminders of God's work making us new through the work of Christ applied by the Spirit.

Why Did God Make You?

God did not make you to be a minister. God made you to know him, glorify him, and to enjoy him forever. Your calling to ministry is not the same as your calling to saving faith in Jesus Christ. Few people who are Christians are called to ministry. A calling to a particular work within and to the church is not your purpose for being alive or your purpose for being alive in Christ.

This is why faithful ministry must begin with your authentic self. It is natural to tie your Christian identity to your particular calling with phrases like "I am a pastor" or "I am a missionary." Though these phrases seem harmless enough, it is important to remember that your ultimate identity is found in Christ and this existed long before you responded to any call to Christian ministry. In Gen 1:26–27 God created humanity in his own image. Man and woman were both formed by God for the express purpose of finding their true identity in relation to God. Bearing the image of God in its fullness is humanity's ultimate aim. In Colossians we are called to grow up into maturity in Christ, who is said to be the "image of the invisible God" (Col 1:15). In other words, we are created to grow up into maturity (Col 3:10). Jesus Christ is the final Adam, the human being fully and perfectly expressing the image of God. Having existed in the image of the man made from dust, we are created for the purpose of identity in Christ and maturity in him (1 Cor 15:47–49).

Our ultimate purpose is not ministry, it's maturity.

How Did God Design You?

You are not merely made for the purpose of maturity in Christ, but you are designed in a particular and unique way. God made you with strengths and weaknesses. But also, your life has shaped your physical, mental, and emotional states. Do you stutter when you speak? Were you in an accident that caused a physical disability? Are you dyslexic? Has a traumatic experience in your life left you scarred emotionally? You are more than the DNA you received when you were knit in your mother's womb. The "you" that you know today is the result of nature and nurture, as it were. God's design of your specific humanity happened in the womb and in the world you have inhabited for the years since your birth.

There may be plenty of things you would like to change about yourself. You may wish you had not been born blind. Or wish you had paid attention in school when people were learning to read. You might regret drug abuse which damaged your mind. You may be the victim of abuse and suffer from PTSD. But any and all of the characteristics which make up your current state of affairs are not impediments to ministry. Something may impede your own, or someone else's, picture of what ministry should be, but none of them are necessarily impediments from you becoming who God calls you to be.

A graduate from the seminary where we both teach is Daniel Ritchie.[1] Daniel was born with no arms. After years of struggling to find his identity while contending with his disability, Daniel became a Christian and discovered his calling: to preach the gospel. Serving Jesus through ministry emerged from finding his identity in Jesus. Today he faithfully ministers in churches throughout the country, helping people of all abilities discover the life-changing message of Jesus.

Who Is the Authentic "You"?

God's call on your life to ministry is not in spite of who you are. Instead, it is to use who you are and who you have become to show himself to others. God does, in fact, intend to use the authentic you. As Paul reminded the believers in Corinth, "Consider your calling: Not many were wise from a human perspective, not many powerful, not many of noble birth. Instead, God has chosen what is foolish in the world to shame the wise, and God has chosen what is weak in the world to shame the strong" (1 Cor 1:26–27). God uses the weak to confound the wise. You must resist the temptation to "appear to be" rather than to *be.* God has not placed you in a ministry assignment because of your potential for

[1] For his story see Daniel Ritchie, *My Affliction for His Glory: Living Out Your Identity in Christ* (Bellingham, WA: Kirkdale, 2018).

ministry. Instead, it is because the authentic "you" fits the current assignment. Ministers may spend all of their time trying to become a different person, when the person they already are is who God intends to use. When God called Moses, the man focused on his inabilities and what he wished he could do better. But the Lord reminded him that what Moses viewed as weaknesses didn't surprise the Lord. In fact, God said, "Who placed a mouth on humans? Who makes a person mute or deaf, seeing or blind? Is it not I, the Lord?" (Exod 4:11).

Every ministry leader is an individual with unique gifts and a unique calling. Each ministry is shaped by the distinct combination of the pastor's experiences, skills, gifts, and personality. Resist the urge to shift focus from the unique calling on your life to your congregation. Recognizing that you are the minister for this time and this church is to acknowledge the Spirit of God as the source of your ministry; you are simply a vessel for him to use.

Who You Are, Not What You Do

Finding your identity in your ability or in the way others respond to your ministry is a surefire way to flame out, flake out, or burn out. What happens when you are no longer "successful" in ministry? What happens when you get sick and can no longer preach? What about when people no longer find you entertaining or appealing? That is the plague of show business—there's a new pastor in town and people flock to hear him preach. What happens when people no longer desire to follow Christ and by many measurements, your ministry no longer flourishes. If your identity in ministry is your ministry, then you set yourself up for disappointment. You also become fertile ground for failure.

When those in ministry define their "work" in terms of accomplishing tasks rather than fulfilling a mission, the soil of service to God and others becomes toxic. A pastor defined by his excellent preaching which, for a season, attracts crowds, may undermine his message through infidelity or dishonesty. Neglecting "who" the preacher is will undo all of his "doing" in a moment. Just as famous musicians have to constantly produce new and better content to remain relevant, ministry that is built on performance requires greater and greater effort, leading to exhaustion and burnout. Ministry rooted in performance rather than in faithfulness is destined for disaster. Caring for your own formation as a follower of Jesus is essential to avoid burnout while serving Jesus.

The Curse of Comparison

It is fine for a professional athlete, business owner, or celebrity to compare themselves to other people. It may not be healthy, but it is not contrary to their vocation. Ministry leaves no room for comparison, but the one doing the work is the Spirit of God, not the minister. First Corinthians 12:4–6 reminds us, "There are different gifts, but the same Spirit. There are different ministries, but the same Lord. And there are different activities, but the same God works all of them in each person." No minister owns the ministry they participate in. That ministry is God's ministry.

The curse of comparison leads to frustration, but it also leads to envy, which leads to bitterness. We become bitter towards God, towards other ministers, towards our church. Why don't the people in our church love us like the people in another church love their pastor? Why do church members respect another minister in our church more than they respect us? If you want to find the quickest path to burnout in ministry, begin to compare your abilities or your success to others.

First, don't compare abilities. You are who you are. There will always be a more talented or gifted minister. Give yourself over fully to serve Jesus by serving others, and God will use even your weaknesses to bring about gospel change in people. While comparison focuses on the minister's strengths, faithful ministry focuses on the Spirit's strength. Your value as a vessel for God's use is not grounded in your ability but in your availability. When you compare yourself to others you are expressing doubt in the power of God to accomplish his own purposes.

Second, don't compare results. Bodies, bucks, and buildings do not signal success in ministry. That's not to say fewer converts, bankrupt churches, or crumbling building are a sign of faithful ministry either. It's better to remember that ministry is about making disciples, not gathering a crowd. A church of poor people is no less honoring to God than a church of wealthy people. Government agencies and wealthy corporations build buildings all the time without fulfilling the Great Commission or the Great Commandment. Strive for faithfulness to the call rather than fruitfulness in your work.

Third, don't compare appreciation. This may be the hardest comparison to avoid. Everyone appreciates being appreciated. Your love language doesn't need to be words of affirmation to value those words of affirmation. Don't be jealous of people who are affirmed more than you, when in your church or other churches. Do I please God or man? Strive to honor God and his work in Jesus Christ in your ministry. At the end of the day ask whether or not your ministry reflects the grace, kindness, and mercy of the gospel. Ask whether Jesus has been exalted, whether the Spirit has worked freely, and whether the Father has been lifted up. And ask those questions with humility, not with pride. You don't serve so that Jesus will appreciate you any more than you serve so that other people will appreciate you. You minister because God is worthy of your faithful service and people are in desperate need for the gospel ministry to which you have been called. Don't take pride in being "better" and don't become defeated by being "worse" than someone else. Consider the words of Jesus in Luke 17:10, "In the same way, when you have done all that you were commanded, you should say, 'We are unworthy servants; we've only done our duty.'" You are not an NFL coach competing against other coaches for the Super Bowl title. You are one minister among many cooperating to help people know Jesus. The minister in another church, whether well-known or unknown, is not your competition. That minister is your teammate. If you are jealous of their notoriety or condescending because of your own, you are not a good teammate.

Being a Truth-Doer as Well as a Truth-Teller

Ministers can far too easily come to practice truth-telling without truth-doing. So much emphasis is placed on the messages pastors preach, the lessons ministers teach, or the confessions Christians make that the practice of the Christian faith can be forgotten. The book of James admonishes us to not just be hearers (or even preachers) of the Word of God, but to be doers of the Word (Jas 1:22). It is certainly important that we watch closely our doctrine, the content of our teaching. But it is equally important that we watch our lives closely as well (see chapter 5). We cannot preach the gospel with compulsion without also living the gospel with confidence in its life-changing nature.

God's call to ministry is a call to a life of serving others. That service entails proclamation of a message, but it equally involves our actions towards others in full expression of that message. It is not enough for us to simply tell people they should serve one another; *we must likewise serve one another.* Ministers serve Jesus by serving other people.

Resist the urge to make ministry solely what you say. If ministry is just what you teach, then you can easily become a hypocrite. Too many pastors we have known started down a path to flaming out of ministry by seeing themselves as *leaders* through their words rather than *servants* through their actions. Jesus washed his disciples' feet while proclaiming to them the kingdom of God. Serving Jesus means becoming a servant of people. Avoid having a dead faith. Have one that is living. And this becomes the example to others of what it means to follow Christ.

Learn to minister in the way God has designed you. Fidelity to God's design of your life, through your genes and your experiences, demonstrates a confidence in God, a trust in his plan and purpose. But refusing to be a "truth-doer," both in terms of practicing the message you preach and doing so in a way that is consistent with your own personal identity in Christ, creates the environment for subtle dishonesty in other areas of your life as well. Do not try to conceal God's design. Be who God made you to be.

Finally, be authentically Christian. You are not perfect, so do not conceal your vulnerabilities. This does not mean you put every sin on display; that would be foolish for anyone, not just ministers. Instead, it means to be honest about God's sanctifying work in your life. Do not strive to make people believe you are better than you really are. When you grieve, let others grieve with you. When you sin against someone, apologize and seek forgiveness. Where there is a broken relationship, strive to mend that relationship. Tell the truth and live the truth. Your own transformation by the gospel will be a model of Christian maturity and a confirmation of the gospel's truthfulness. Represent for people what you are trying to shepherd them to become. As Paul said to the Corinthian church, "Imitate me, as I also imitate Christ" (1 Cor 11:1).

You Are the Minister Where You Are

Remember that God has you in a ministry assignment for his purposes. You are not in a certain church because you are the most gifted person they could have found. There are probably many others who could do a better "job" at that church. But you are there because God will use you as a useful vessel, designed at this specific moment to be the minister of that congregation. To compare yourself to what someone is doing in a different church is to disregard God's plan woven into the fabric of your church.

It may be easy to think of someone who would be better than you in your ministry position. It may also be easy to imagine that you might be better at your ministry if you were different. You might be frustrated with who you are or even where you are. Some ministers are inclined to appear different so they can find another place to serve!

It's easy to become disillusioned with ministry if you are pretentious. Pretending to be someone you are not leads to disappointment and frustration. You may have heard it said, "Dress for the job you want and not the one you have." It may work if you are trying to move up or move on, but ministry happens where you are, not necessarily where you want to be. God placed you in a ministry assignment that fits with how he has designed you. You may desire a different assignment. But Paul says to pursue the greatest gift of love (1 Cor 12:31, 13:13). Grow where you are planted. Serve where you are right now. Learn contentedness in ministry. When I was a young minister, I always wanted to be in the next spot. I was never truly content with the current ministry. And, at times, it caused me to look past immediate ministry opportunities in search of future ones. How many times did I miss the blessing of fruitful and faithful ministry in the pursuit of sheep in a different pasture?! I can't help but think that I became frustrated and burned out in ministries because of that failure to till the ground around me and teach the people in my immediate surroundings.

That's not to say there are not times for moving pastures, but difficulty alone is not a sufficient reason to abandon people. There are good reasons why you should consider a different ministry assignment. Walking in wisdom, hearing the counsel of other believers, and observing the Spirit's work in and through you can help you discern when it is appropriate to begin a new season of ministry in a different place (for example, when the ministry is counter-productive to your Christian maturity). Just because ministry is hard does not mean it has to distract you from growing in Christ. When you can no longer walk with people to encourage one another to love and good works, it may be time to minister elsewhere.

It is also likely you should change ministry assignments when you no longer have people to serve. A pastor who is asked to leave a church will, obviously, need a new ministry assignment. A teacher in the church may no longer have people who want to attend their Bible study. You may have a sense of an inward call to a particular ministry, but if the "outward" call does not exist, you need to identify the place where people want you as their minister.

Finally, you cannot stay in a place when your continued ministry would be harmful to other people. Hurt people hurt people. It's true of ministers as well. We've seen far too many instances of bitter ministers causing harm to other people. Time away is better than time spent bringing ill repute on the gospel or allowing bitterness to bring irreparable harm to your relationships. When you are hurt, you are vulnerable to hurting others. It is entirely appropriate to take time away from a ministry, or even away from the ministry altogether, in order to find healing. We are hoping in this book to help mitigate some of the hurt and burnout that leads to a desire for a break from ministry. But there are indeed times when you may not be healthy enough to stay. Be wise and step away before causing harm to a church or people in the church.

The Rot of Comparison

Comparing yourself to others in ministry is truly a curse. You forfeit the blessing of enjoying God's good work in your life, in your ministry, and in your church when you turn attention away from God's faithfulness and to your own sense of achievement. Comparison kills in ways that make a lifetime of faithful ministry impossible. How does the curse of comparison harm you and your ministry?

Partners Become Competitors

Paul writes to the Corinthians that one of their great sins was identifying themselves with particular leaders or ministers rather than with the single community God made them to be. In their desire to one-up one another, they had in essence made partners in the ministry appear to be competitors with one another. One group identifies with Paul, another with Apollos, and so on (1 Cor 1:10–17). Partners in the ministry had divided themselves from one another through their allegiances. This division is counterproductive to faithful ministry. Do not give in to comparison that becomes competition.

When you begin to compare yourself to others in ministry, you quickly end up trying to outperform or outshine other ministers or churches. It becomes hard to pray for or cheer for the fruitfulness of another church when you are secretly hoping for their demise. Imagine feeling a sense of disappointment when another church posts about their recent baptisms on social media because you are jealous of their "success." In your heart, you have now set yourself *against* other pastors because of envy. Alternatively, if you are the one posting about recent "successes," you act with pride toward other churches. Either way, you have sinned against that church, turning them into a competitor rather than a partner in the gospel.

You also create in yourself an unhealthy pressure to outperform other pastors or churches. Your measure of success becomes only those measurable stats you can post for the others to see. Now you create stress for yourself that can erode the joy of ministry and contribute to burnout. An unhealthy pursuit of the appearance of success makes ministry a burden rather than a blessing and turns fellow ministers into enemies instead of friends. This desire to outperform others can easily lead to viewing church members as means to your own selfish ends, helping you achieve a status to make a name for yourself. Resist the urge to compete with other pastors and churches for the sake of your own ministry.

Questioning Your Calling

Constant comparison with other pastors can quickly erode your sense of calling by leading to fits of despair and feelings of inadequacy. Because the core of comparison in ministry is judging success solely by external metrics, any failure to achieve those quantifiable goals will be interpreted as a failure in ministry. Some ministers believe the only "successful" churches are big churches. When you see other churches that have a higher attendance or a bigger budget and you conclude they are more faithful than your church, you have fallen victim to this curse. Once you begin to question God's call to your particular ministry, you will soon see any effectiveness you have in that ministry begin to wane. You will feel insecure and inadequate, forgetting that God is the source of a church's fruit, not you, which leads to a final consequence.

Ministering in the Flesh

Once you give in to constant comparison, you will soon lose a sense of the church as God's church. Pastors can easily begin to consider the church's ministry as dependent on their own ingenuity, effort, or charisma. Programs suddenly become more important than people. The pastor may begin to cultivate a following around himself of loyalists and supporters. No longer is the goal of ministry seeing people glorify God and enjoy him; it is now to provide the pastor with bragging rights or a sense of accomplishment. Sadly, as long as the pastor who is ministering by the power of the flesh rather than the power of the Spirit is getting the results he wants, his ministry may continue unabated. But eventually, either the pastor may be crushed by the lack of spiritual vitality in his ministry, or the results stop and the pastor becomes overwhelmed by a sense of failure. Either way, the pastor, not to mention the church, loses his way. Avoiding burnout requires resisting the urge to compare oneself to other ministers.

The pastor is not the only casualty of the curse of comparison; the church suffers as well. Congregations of disciples who are participating in the Great Commission realize their purpose: make disciples from all nations. Honest and genuine Christians who desire to share in the work of the ministry, build authentic Christian community, and see other people come to know Jesus are not participating in the church to aid the pastor's reputation or build his self-esteem. Instead, they are serving because they love Jesus and love people.

As churches shift their focus to only seeking tangible metrics, they will lose their own sense of spiritual vitality. Pastors who lead churches to serve in the flesh rather than the Spirit not only cause harm to the people, but they create confusion in the minds of the congregation about the purpose of their ministry. If their goal is only to draw a crowd or build a beautiful space or participate in self-congratulatory celebrations, then where is the gospel? The gospel may become relegated to the corners, or even to the past. Rather than existing for the purpose of making disciples, the church may reinterpret its purpose as simply achieving certain results. Whenever the church loses its way, the people no longer share in the blessing of the gospel.

The curse of comparison also causes the church to neglect its own unique contribution to the gospel's progress. 1 Corinthians 12 reminds us that the Spirit brings to the church people who make it unique. There are gifts at your church that might be redundant or useless at another church. When you fail to lean into the uniqueness of your congregation due to unhealthy comparison and competition with another congregation, those unique gifts are neglected.

Resisting the Temptation to Compare

Comparison in ministry is a dead end. You must strive to resist that temptation, as strong as it might be. Reject the voice that says your comparison is healthy comparison. In ministry, comparison is nearly always rooted in either envy or pride, both of which are deadly diseases for faithful ministry leaders. If you give in to comparison, you will inevitably experience the rot that results from it. So how can you resist that temptation?

First, anchor your ministry in your unique calling. Throughout your ministry there will be times when returning to your calling to ministry will help you combat the immediate challenge. When you are tempted to compare, remember God called you to serve him. When you forget that you are serving Jesus, you may end up serving some other end.

Second, cultivate your own spiritual life. Ministry is a spiritual exercise. Like with any temptation, you are being drawn away by your own desire to be recognized or to appear successful. Respond to that temptation like you would any other: turn to Jesus. Set your mind on things above. Immerse yourself in the Scriptures. Focus on regular times of prayer. Remind yourself that you belong to God and live for him. There is nothing that will calm your envious soul like the awareness of the presence of the Holy Spirit in your life.

Third, identify where God is working in your current ministry. Rather than comparing your church to the church down the road, look for spiritual fruit in your own church. Remember the narrative of the widow's offering. Jesus celebrates small spiritual fruit just as joyfully as large spiritual fruit. Find the sources of joy in your church and celebrate them. When my children were learning to walk, my wife and I celebrated one small step followed by a tumble to the ground. What would we have missed if we had been watching the neighbor's older child ride a bike instead of our own child learning to walk? It is possible that people are learning to walk all around your church and you are too busy being envious of another church just because they have people riding bicycles. And if you cannot see God at work in your current ministry, then maybe it is because you are trying to be someone other than who God called you to be. Focus on where you are, not where someone else is.

Fourth, celebrate other ministers and ministries. This can be difficult if you are not maturing in Christ yourself. Choose to rejoice in what God is doing in other churches, starting with praying for other churches. When you see something praiseworthy happening at another church, stop and give thanks to God. Then, consider sending an email, a text, or a handwritten note to the pastor to encourage him. From the outside you see a tangible metric, but growing churches often have unseen challenges. Gratitude and encouragement go a long way to shape our own sensitivity to God's ongoing work.

Finally, accurately measure health in yourself, your ministry, and your church. Health is measured in faithfulness. Ask people to share what God is doing in their lives. Report on more than just standard metrics; report on spiritual growth and faithfulness in ministry. Celebrate God's faithfulness to your church. When a child goes from crawling to walking, we have a party. Why shouldn't we also celebrate spiritual advancements as well? As you help your congregation define success in terms of faithfulness, they will make sure you do not forget it either.

{ CHAPTER 4 }

Lifelong Growth for Lifelong Ministry

> I am the vine; you are the branches. The one who remains in me and I in him produces much fruit, because you can do nothing without me.
>
> —John 15:5

Principle: Faithful ministry requires ongoing growth.

Introduction

One of the hobbies Steve and I (Scott) share in common is woodworking. We like to build furniture, smaller pieces, and even artwork from wood. Quite often, in the middle of a project, things start getting more difficult. The cuts are not as clean, and the pieces do not fit together as they should. One of my first instincts is to push harder or pound the tool with more force. This never works. Usually, the problem is that all the previous work has dulled the saw. This problem can never be fixed by applying more force or working harder. The only solution is taking time to properly sharpen the tool.

Those of us in Christian ministry understand the frustration. We have a vision. We work hard. We see progress, but then, despite our best efforts, things stall. Numbers decline, interest wanes, and people stop responding. Then, accompanying this lagging progress, doubt creeps in. We work harder but don't achieve the results we'd hoped for. Exhaustion settles in, and we are ripe for burnout or something worse.

During the 2020 pandemic lockdown and accompanying social unrest, I (Scott) became burdened for pastors and those serving in local church ministry. We all heard stories of serious emotional and spiritual struggles. This led dozens of pastors to contemplate stepping away from ministry. In response to these statistics, I wrote an open letter to pastors and published it on the *Lifeway Voices* website. In the article, I sought to highlight the importance of the pastor's work, and I begged them not to quit at the moment when those of us in the church needed them most. I encouraged church leaders to step back and get refreshed for their emotional health and longevity in ministry. I wrote, "Take a break . . . start a hobby, cook a steak, dig a hole and put a flower in it."[1]

This letter gained some traction in a few social media circles. It was even translated into other languages. As a

---

[1] D. Scott Hildreth, "Dear Pastor, Please Don't Quit on Us Now," *Lifeway Voices*, September 14, 2020, https://voices.lifeway.com/church-ministry-leadership/dear-pastor-please-dont-quit-on-us-now/.

result, pastors and church leaders responded with different messages, suggestions, and questions. One message still haunts me. This brother reacted negatively to my encouragement to step back. He pointed out that he served as pastor of a single-staff church. He had a full calendar and a hurting church. He didn't have the luxury to take a break.

I felt his pain. I also prayed for this brother and the thousands of others in similar situations. This feeling of being too busy to step away and sharpen our tools indicates that we are headed for trouble.

In this chapter, we want to discuss the importance of continual growth and staying sharp throughout the years of ministry. While it is true that we are not in complete control of what happens around us, taking some determined and disciplined steps for ongoing growth will help you survive, be more fruitful in ministry, and avoid temptation and sin. This chapter will also point out three areas of growth that will help prevent burnout and will also give some practical tips along the way.

What Is Growth?

As we begin, perhaps it is best to answer the question, What do we mean by growth? In some sense, growth is so natural that it doesn't need to be defined. After all, when a young couple has a baby, growth is expected. Babies gain weight, get taller/longer, learn skills, and eventually start caring for themselves. Growth isn't forced; it is what it means to be alive. Growth is perhaps the most fundamental characteristic of any living thing.

Several years ago, I planted a garden from seeds. I wanted to try my hand at homemade salsa. I planted different colored peppers with varying levels of heat. I also planted some onions, tomatoes, and cilantro. After a month of nursing the seeds inside my house, I moved the plants outside. Within a few weeks, they took off—the plants got bigger and produced more fruit than I could process. I ended up giving away more than I used.

The interesting thing about this garden was that, even though growth happened naturally, if I had left things to themselves, the fruit would not have developed as it did. Without some sticks and trellises, the plants would have fallen to the ground, where the bugs and moisture would have destroyed them. To have a healthy garden, I needed to take practical steps to shape the growth for maximum yield. Lifelong ministry and ongoing fruitfulness are a bit like this garden. We "grow" as life happens. We get older and have more experiences. We will learn things along the way. But growth that sustains our ministry over the long haul requires some planning and ongoing effort.

Let's shift metaphors for a moment. Because we live in a fallen world, the natural pull of our culture is away from godliness and a lifestyle that supports long-term ministry. Let's call this new enemy "the drift." This enemy raises its ugly head when we ignore the drag in our society and float into stagnation or sin.

We grew up on the Alabama Gulf Coast, the home of the most beautiful beaches in the world. Anytime we go to the beach, we know it is necessary to put an ice chest or umbrella on the beach where we first wade into the water. We have learned through the years that the constant movement of the current pulls you away from that home base. The regular rhythm of the ocean slowly but steadily drags you down the beach.

The frightening thing about this drift is that we are usually unaware of the movement. Whether fishing, wading, tossing a football, or floating on a raft, the slow and steady current moves us along. Then, before you know it, you end up in a place where the water is over your head, or you could end up hundreds of yards down the beach. The journey back is much more arduous than it would have been if you'd stayed close to home base. Because the water and beach look the same, the only indicator you have of movement are the things you place on the beach as a reminder of where things started.

Our lives mimic this beach experience. The current of our culture and the daily grind of ministry is a continual pull. We may not realize it, but our hearts and minds are being dragged away. Without some intentionality, we can drift into dangerous territory where temptation drags us down. We don't even realize we are being pulled, but in one quick moment, we are in deep water, going under.

Or, if we aren't paying attention to the currents around us, we may look up one day and discover that we have drifted far from where we started. Our passions have waned, or our vision has dimmed. We find ourselves overwhelmed. Maybe we know the way back, but sheer exhaustion tempts us to give up rather than do the necessary work to correct our course and get back where we started. These consequences of this drift leave us vulnerable to burnout or worse.

Because we live in a broken world, "the drift" is always present. Not only does this great enemy affect us, but it also influences those around us and those in our churches. We must always be alert. This is Paul's caution to the Galatians, watching our for yourselves so that you also won't be tempted" (Gal 6:1).

One of the ways to guard against these dangers, fighting to overcome stagnation and drift, is by prioritizing growth. The rest of this chapter is designed to help you plant a marker on the beach to monitor the drift and create sufficient trellises in your life for fruitfulness and stability for life-long ministry.

A Biblical Outline for Areas of Growth

To provide a workable structure for growth, we will draw on the description of how three biblical characters grew: Jesus, John the Baptist, and Samuel. To be fair, these passages are not instructional, and they were not written as a way to guide growth. However, they do give us some common categories we can use as an outline for the chapter and some tangible handles to consider as we evaluate our growth and plan for ways to stay sharp and avoid burnout.

- Jesus:
  - "And Jesus increased in wisdom and stature, and in favor with God and with people" (Luke 2:52).
- John the Baptist:
  - "The child grew up and became strong in spirit, and he was in the wilderness until the day of his public appearance to Israel" (Luke 1:80).
- Samuel:
  - "The boy Samuel grew in stature and in favor with the Lord and with people" (1 Sam 2:26).

In each of these descriptive passages, different writers describe how these young men grew in several key areas: intellectually, physically, and spiritually. As we consider drift and areas of growth, we will keep these three categories in mind.

Intellectual Growth

- What was the last book you read or podcast you listened to that challenged your thinking?
- Have you changed your mind or behavior recently because of something you learned?
- What new ministry or leadership insight have you gleaned recently that influenced how you engage in your work?

Each of these statements, though framed differently, really asks a single question, Are you in an intellectual rut? Most of us can remember a season of intellectual growth. Perhaps it was when you were in college, seminary, or graduate school. Maybe it was when you first entered your ministry assignment and realized there was so much you hadn't learned. During these seasons, we feel mentally sharp and motivated for the day's challenges. Curiosity drives us to read, learn, and apply new lessons to problems.

Then, life happened. You learned the basic skills, earned the degree, or simply lost the sense of desperation that drove you to search for new answers. In some ways, this is okay; it is to be expected. Growth happened, and you currently live at a new level. It would be a shame if we had to continue reviewing the basics. On the other hand, if we are not careful, we will stagnate—content with what we have learned and the ability to perform our duties at the current level.

Let's say you decide to pick up a new hobby—woodworking. In the early days, you spend money and time acquiring tools and new skills. You read books, watch videos, and may even join online groups. You probably spend as much time learning about woodworking as you do working with wood. It's exhilarating. New skills, shiny tools, and even some completed projects start to stack up.

But in time, you have learned the basics skills and built a workshop of necessary tools. Your sense of desperation lessens, and you settle into a routine, using skills to create new and better furniture or other wood projects. It would be unfair to think that you needed to sustain the frantic learning pace of those early days.

You have acquired the basic knowledge for the tasks at hand. However, you haven't learned all there is to know. At this point, skills and knowledge are more challenging and slower to perfect. You have learned to cut a board, but can you cut two boards so that they fit perfectly together? You learned to make simple furniture, but what about furniture that transcends functionality and approaches craft or art?

I heard a story about a young pastor who invited one of his ministry heroes to speak at his church. The day arrived, and the pastor drove his hero back to his office to get ready for the event. When they returned to the church, the older minister walked into the young pastor's office and started browsing his library. He looked at commentaries and systematic theology texts. He pulled down practical ministry books and skimmed the pages of other contemporary leadership texts.

"Can I help you find something?"

"No," the older man said. "When I visit another pastor's office I like to look at the publication dates of his books. I just wanted to see when you started dying."

Let's be fair; not every new book or current topic is worth your time and attention. However, ongoing intellectual growth is necessary to overcome the malaise that can lead to burnout. Lifelong learning stimulates creativity, challenges misplaced assumptions, and creates intellectual energy about your work and ministry.

In addition to the ministry's spiritual and emotional aspects, we must also make intellectual investments in the work. We need to plan, reflect, and compose better ways of teaching the gospel's message and explaining the truth of the Christian faith. Intellectual laziness can far too easily lead to laxity in our thinking about the gospel we are called to lead people further into. Failure to grow intellectually means failure to pursue the knowledge of God, which is the foundation of our own lives and ministries.

Longevity in ministry requires us to adapt to the changing context in which we live. It is tempting to do what has worked in the past or to copy the ministry practices of others. This lack of creativity leaves us in a rut and vulnerable to boredom. This is why it is vital to continue to develop intellectually. The eternal gospel is good news for all people of all time, but our changing context and shifting culture should push us to expand our knowledge.

Physical Growth

- How's your health?
- Do you ever think about what you eat, how much you rest, or physical exercise?
- More importantly, do you ever do anything about these things?

Our culture is obsessed with physical health. Advertisements for diet pills, gym memberships, and miracle cures fill our televisions and social media feeds. This demonstrates that far too many people seek security and hope in this world and are overly fixated on their physical bodies. However, their unhealthy obsession is no excuse for the neglect many of us show our physical health.

When I reflect on the importance of physical growth and health, I am haunted by the final words of Scottish pastor, Robert Murray M'Cheyne. On his death bed at age twenty-nine, he wrote, "God gave me a message to deliver and a horse to ride [speaking of his own body]. Alas, I have killed the horse and can no longer deliver the message." Most of us are not given bodies that can be transformed into bodybuilders or professional athletes. However, God has given us a physical body to serve him with, and our stewardship of this gift is an essential factor in sustaining ministry. Our long-term success in ministry is directly connected to our physical bodies.

Frankly, we are too well-educated to be as negligent of our physical well-being as many of us are.

1. We know about the food pyramid and how eating affects mental and physical health.

2. We know that a sedentary lifestyle is a quick way to more significant physical issues.
3. We know proper rest not only keeps us physically healthy; it also makes us more pleasant to be around and more sensitive to the needs of others.
4. We also know that the Bible gives us clear directives about properly stewarding our bodies and even reminds us that "bodily training is of some value" (1 Tim 4:8, ESV).

At the same time, the demands of ministry can create problems for each of these areas of health:

1. We often eat at odd hours and are not always in control of what we eat.
2. Ministry requires long hours of sitting to study, travel, talking with people, or meetings.
3. The role's demands require late nights and early mornings and allow very little time for real rest.
4. The duties of ministry often undermine our ability to pursue physical health.

At the end of the day, you only have one body to use in service to the Lord. When we fail to take care of it, not only are we poor stewards of the gift and tool God gave us, we also hinder our usefulness for God's work. We are integrated beings; this means that our physical bodies influence our minds and emotions. Failure to take care of our physical bodies can also lead to burnout. Be determined not to allow mistakes in this area impact your ministry usefulness long-term.

Spiritual Growth

- How is your devotional life?
- What sin are you refusing to kill, or what temptation do you continually flirt with?
- Are there people you are not loving well or forgiving completely?

Ongoing spiritual formation isn't a luxury, it's a necessity for ministry success. Jesus emphasized this in John 15 when he told his disciples, "I am the vine; you are the branches. The one who remains in me and I in him produces much fruit, because you can do nothing without me" (John 15:5). In this, the last of Jesus's self-identifying "I am" statements, he makes a crucial connection between ministry success and our relationship with him. Charles Spurgeon, in a sermon on this passage, notes, "You may *talk* a good deal without him; you may hold congresses, and conferences, and conventions; but *doing* is another matter. Without Jesus, you can *talk* any quantity; but without him, you can *do* nothing. The most eloquent discourse without Him will be all a bottle of smoke."[2]

The problem, however, is that this verse does not seem true. We aren't suggesting that the Bible is wrong; instead, we acknowledge that our assessment may be off regarding the importance of our Christian growth. In ministry, we can produce things that seem important and for which we get accolades. However, if we do them apart from Christ, these

[2] Charles Spurgeon, "Without Christ – Nothing," in *The Treasury of the Bible* (Grand Rapids: Baker, 1988), 557.

"things" are actually "nothing." This feeling of emptiness eventually catches up with us and contributes to burnout.

Christian ministry is spiritual work and cannot be reduced to a series of well-planned activities or business principles. The needs around us far exceed our capacity, and this constant pressure takes a daily toll on our well-being. This feeling of inadequacy is amplified by the spiritual expectations of ministry to provide biblical counsel for and solutions for a myriad of life's problems. Like the apostle Paul, we carry the "daily pressure . . . concern for all the churches" (2 Cor 11:28). For these reasons, we must minister out of the overflow of our spiritual lives, drawing deep from the well of the Spirit. Burnout happens when ministry depletes our reserves, leaving us dry and empty.

One of the dangers related to the significance of spiritual growth and ministry is to downplay its importance. However, an equally problematic attitude exists: reducing spiritual formation to a string of tasks on a to-do list. Several years ago, I heard a conference speaker ask, "Which one of these statements are indicators of spiritual maturity?" He proceeded to list things like:

- Regular times of prayer each day
- Memorization of large portions of Scripture
- Regular attendance to worship services
- Actively seeking to win people to the faith
- Intentionally discerning false teaching, confronting the teacher, and correcting the mistake
- Daily Scripture intake
- Deep concern for personal holiness and the holiness of others

- Courage in the face of public ridicule

At the end of his list, I had checked off nearly every statement. Imagine my surprise when he said, "This list is a description of the Pharisees." That conference was over thirty years ago, and I still remember realizing that spiritual growth cannot be measured by a list of activities. It is measured by abiding in Christ and growth in Christlikeness.

Spiritual disciplines are important for our spiritual formation; however, they cannot be the measure of growth. In his book *Underneath the Unpredictable Plant,* Eugene Peterson provides a helpful description of spiritual growth. Our lives, he observes, are like a garden. In a garden, all the necessary elements for growth come from God: rain, sun, soil, nutrients, etc. Likewise, the joy, hardships, ministry moments, family, and even the mundane drudgery of life come from God and create the environment for God-given growth.

Spiritual disciplines, he observes, are like gardening tools. Each serves a purpose for cultivation. "Tools," he writes, "must be used according to what the plant and soil need; enthusiasm with a shovel will destroy a tender tomato plant when all that was needed was the deft application of a hoe to loosen the soil."[3] No one would measure the health of a garden by describing how often they water it or how aggressively they pull weeds. We evaluate growth by the health of the plant and the fruit it produces.

As we observed earlier, Jesus tells us that our fruitfulness is determined by one factor: abiding in him (John 15).

---

[3] Eugene H. Peterson, *Under the Unpredictable Plant: An Exploration in Vocational Holiness* (Grand Rapids: Eerdmans, 1992), 109.

Since this is true, the reverse is also true; the test of our abiding in Jesus can be evaluated by producing fruit. What are some indicators of fruit production? Here are a few from Jesus's discourse in John 15.

- We are growing in the word and prayer (John 15:7).
- Our affection for God and his glory, not our own, is growing (John 15:9).
- We seek to obey Christ's teachings (John 15:10).
- Joy is growing (John 15:11).
- We love others (John 15:12).
- We endure hostility and persecution (John 15:18).

Now, we could add to this list things like the fruit of evangelism and the fruit of the Spirit. But the point of this section is not to heap guilt on ourselves. Instead, this reminds us that spiritual growth is not a series of tasks; rather, it is our participation with the Spirit as he completes the work he started in us through Christ.

If we reduce spiritual formation to a task list, we feed into what Peterson calls "consumer mentality," where we reduce our activities (especially spiritual disciplines) to some form of cost/benefit analysis. This is a sure path to burnout because our spiritual growth is not purely dependent on us. When we take on a task that is too large, we will surely feel like failures in the end—we will want to give up. Failing to abide in Christ results in empty religious tasks that leave us tired, burdened, and empty. Spiritual emptiness, along with mental and physical unhealth, leads us to faithless and fruitless human endeavors rather than faithful gospel ministry.

Spiritual Growth is a Lifetime Investment

1. Invest in Spiritual Formation and Healthy Use of Disciplines

Earlier in this chapter, we provided a vision of spiritual formation that suggested spiritual disciplines were tools for cultivation but not the measurement of our growth. Some may take this as a suggestion that these disciplines are optional. Nothing could be further from the truth.

Disciplines like Scripture intake (reading, listening, memorization, study), prayer, worship, journaling, meditation, fellowship, service, fasting, silence, and celebration have proven to be vitally important for spiritual growth through the centuries of church history. It would be the height of arrogance to assume that we no longer need to engage in these time-tested and scripturally-prescribed activities.

Our encouragement is that we invest in these in ways that promote growth. Donald Whitney notes, "Christlikeness is the goal, the reason we should practice the Disciplines. Without this purpose in our practice, the performance . . . is vain and nothing more than an empty husk of godliness."[4] Growth requires effort and the disciplines are our chief tools for maturity.

Some disciplines should be a regular part of our lives because they are commanded in Scripture and are important for connecting us with God and his people. We are thinking about Bible intake, prayer, and worship. These disciplines form a daily/weekly regimen that keeps us

---

[4] Donald S. Whitney, *Spiritual Disciplines for the Christian Life*, rev. ed. (Colorado Springs: NavPress, 2014), 9.

working in the garden of our souls. Other disciplines can, and should, be incorporated into our lives with consistency and also as a means to address specific areas of growth or spiritual needs. For example, if you find yourself distracted by the noise of life and are unable to quiet yourself and hear from the Lord, a regular practice of silence and solitude may be the exercise that strengthens you in this area.

As we keep in mind that our spiritual growth and formation is our participation with the Spirit, we can keep a healthy perspective and implementation of these tools in our life. In an instant gratification culture, people often neglect the basic spiritual disciplines that maintain growth over their lives. Our encouragement is that you make time in your schedule to apply these time-proven exercises as the means for spiritual maturity.

2. Read Widely

It has been said, "Readers are leaders." This may be true, but this depends on what you read and what you do with the information you acquire. Most people in ministry have a collection of books: some we have read, some we plan to read, and some we have acquired for any number of reasons. When we think about reading for growth, what do we have in mind? One of our greatest temptations is narrowing our reading to topics we are already familiar with or authors who affirm our beliefs. This is not the kind of reading that promotes growth.

Albert Mohler, president of The Southern Baptist Theological Seminary, provides some helpful suggestions for planned reading that promotes ongoing maturity and growth.[5] First, he advises readers to develop a plan. A good plan promotes variety and helps the reader budget for books. Mohler suggests creating categories that will focus your study and keep you sharp in several key areas. His include: theology, biblical studies, church life, history, cultural studies, and literature. Now, your categories may be different and may change depending on life's situations. However, having a plan and reading through your plan will ensure progress and fresh thinking.

Next, he suggests reading deeply. He encourages readers to dive deeply, reading works related to major sections of Scripture. This study could include commentaries, sermons, or other books that help with the deep study of Scripture. Mohler also recommends reading broadly through an entire set of books and choosing an author to read everything written by him or her.

Finally, he recommends that we read for fun. Sometimes, our reading takes us to a place we have never traveled (even a fantasy world); it introduces us to people and situations we might not encounter in our regular walk of life. Reading fiction and non-fiction for fun fuels creativity and helps us avoid burnout.

Some may balk at the encouragement above because it seems like a huge financial expense. It is true that books cost money; however, they are a vital investment in your future and health. At the same time, don't neglect the many

---

[5] R. Albert Mohler, Jr., "Some Thoughts on the Reading of Books," *Albert Mohler*, September 25, 2015, https://albertmohler.com/2015/09/25/some-thoughts-on-the-reading-of-books-3.

ways you can read good books at a library or even forming a reading group—other ministers who read and share books. Not only does this give you an incredible number of books to read, but it also creates a community of readers that can keep you accountable and serve as a sounding board for processing what you have read.

This plan doesn't promise instant growth. Instead, following these principles through the years will ensure that you are growing and are not settling into an intellectual rut. Read well—read widely—read often—when in doubt, read another book.

3. Steward Your Physical Health as a Gift from God and a Tool for Service

Learning to care for our bodies is similar to caring for our vehicles. For our car to fulfill its purpose effectively, it requires regular maintenance. We change the oil, rotate the tires, and check fluid levels. When there is a problem, we address it quickly enough to prevent further damage and the expense that comes with it. You can indeed drive a car without changing the oil. You might do this for quite a while without noticing any damage to the engine. But eventually, you will experience trouble; the engine will break due to a failure to maintain it properly.

Now, you can't always prevent mechanical failure in your car. Sometimes, despite your effort, your engine will blow a head gasket, or some other part will fail. This may be the result of a faulty part or simply long-term wear from use. Whatever the cause, the result is the same: your car is stuck in your driveway.

Your body is much the same way. You cannot prevent all diseases. You cannot help being injured in an accident. But you can give attention to your physical health through checkups, healthy eating, and exercising. We are not suggesting physical health is more important than spiritual growth. In fact, Paul writes, "Bodily training is of some value, godliness is of value in every way, as it holds promise for the present life and also for the life to come" (1 Tim 4:8, ESV). Instead, we want to emphasize that burnout is often the result of bodies or minds weakened by laziness or refusal to practice preventative maintenance.

Being sick is not the same as being sinful. But when we are tired, weak, or ill, we will struggle to fulfill our ministry. Fatigue can make us vulnerable to temptation, emotional swings, and outbursts of anger. So, taking care of the vessel we have been given is vital to longevity and fruitfulness. Take care of your mental and physical health as best as possible.

As we observed earlier in the chapter, most of us are educated enough to make wise decisions about our health. Our encouragement is not to make you feel guilty about your physical limitations or to pressure you into a diet or workout plan. Instead, our concern is that you do not find yourself, like M'Cheyne, in a place of physical compromise and no longer able to perform the duties of your calling. Let's treat our bodies like a gift and a tool, both from the Lord and for his service.

4. Enlist Others to Support You in Your Growth

Because the pull of our culture encourages drift away from growth and godliness, we need some accountability to maintain motivation. Later in this book, we will highlight the importance of friendships. However, here, it is crucial that we remind ourselves that this journey of growth is not a journey we should undertake alone. Spiritual, emotional, and intellectual maturity require participation in relationships with fellow pilgrims journeying through life with one another.

We aren't just asking you to create an accountability group. History has proven that these groups are only moderately effective. You can always be dishonest and deceptive with those you enlist to hold you accountable. If this is your attitude, then the group is counterproductive. But if you are going to win the battle over "the drift" in your life, it is always better to have someone to help you share the load. As we grow in ministry, it benefits us and others, to be in community.

Conclusion

Growth happens. But the growth we discuss in this chapter requires a degree of thought and intentionality. Avoiding burnout requires us to take an honest assessment of the world around us. Recognize its traps and temptations. None of us are immune to the power of the drift or the draw of culture to life in the rut. However, we also recognize that this is not the life we want to live.

The encouragement and guidelines we supply in this chapter can be used by those who already find themselves exhausted and headed for trouble. We hope each reader will recognize the danger and take steps to stay sharp and vigilant for a life-long ministry of fruitfulness and joy.

{ CHAPTER 5 }

God's Not the Only One with a Plan for Your Life

For our struggle is not against flesh and blood,
but against the rulers, against the authorities,
against the cosmic powers of this darkness,
against evil, spiritual forces in the heavens. For
this reason take up the full armor of God, so
that you may be able to resist in the evil day, and
having prepared everything, to take your stand.

—Eph 6:12–13

Principle: Guard your character, it is the only message you have.

Introduction

We have a friend who spent many years in a public ministry position. Part of his ministry passion was to mentor young men and shape them for life changing ministry. He was the kind of person that others sought to emulate. He wrote books, preached sermons, spoke at conferences, and regularly scheduled time for mentorship meetings. Over the years we heard stories of dozens of men who pointed to this brother as their father in the ministry.

Then one dark day the news broke that this man had been caught in a compromising situation. In one moment, everything he had worked to build crashed and, in the words of Jesus, "great was the fall" (Matt 7:27). Almost overnight, books were pulled, conference invitations were revoked, and sermons deleted. Perhaps worst of all, dozens of young men and women were plunged into disillusion and doubt. Some walked away from the ministry and others abandoned the faith entirely.

As we reflected together on the damaging impact of this brother's fall, one thought haunted us. We thought about the old evangelism tract, *The Four Spiritual Laws.* This presentation of the gospel started with the catch phrase, "God Loves you and has a Wonderful Plan for your life." As we discussed this phrase, we were reminded that the Lord is not the only one with a plan for our lives. The enemy also has a plan.

Satan's plan includes enticing you to sin, convincing you that it's ok and no one will ever find out. Then, he will expose your sin as a tool for undermining the gospel and reputation of the body of Christ.

In this chapter, we want to discuss temptation, sin, and the importance of pursuing godliness. We want to highlight areas of life in which ministers are especially vulnerable and provide some encouragement for staying faithful to the Lord. Learning to resist temptation, avoid sin, and submit fully to Christ as Lord are absolutely necessary to perseverance in faithful ministry. Neglecting your spiritual well-being while only cultivating skills and performing tasks will ensure an eventual failure.

Not only does living with hidden sin risk public exposure, it is also a sure path to burnout in ministry. The writer of Hebrews reminds us that sin is a burden: "let us lay aside every hindrance and the sin that so easily ensnares us" (Heb 12:1). Secret sin weighs on the mind and makes us vulnerable to physical and emotional exhaustion. The energy required to live a duplicitous life as a minister far exceeds the energy needed to fulfill one's calling in ministry. Additionally, a sinful lifestyle undermines the very nature of the spiritual formation at the root of a healthy and faithful ministry. Cultivating a life of faithfulness to Christ requires avoiding sin through resisting unhealthy affections as well as forming particular Christian characteristics that undergird discipling others and caring for their spiritual well-being.

Resisting Unhealthy Affections

Having a character that contributes to faithfulness in ministry begins with identifying unhealthy affections that ministers are prone to developing. Sin is always creeping at the door, but there are desires that seem to be particularly prevalent among those in ministry. Recognizing your vulnerability to these unhealthy affections helps you avoid a path that leads to fatigue, failure, and burnout.

Affection for Leisure

Everyone needs rest. The body cannot operate effectively without physical rest. Your mind needs a break from being always engaged. Sufficient sleep is important to proper health. Because of the high-stress nature of ministry, those in ministry need to take time away from their work. Pastors should take vacation time. Every minister should take time off to allow their bodies, minds, and souls to recover. As we explained in chapter four, if you do not care for yourself, you will not be healthy enough for ministry.

But there is a difference between taking time for leisure, like hobbies and vacations, and having such an affection for leisure that you become lazy. There are certainly no vocations where laziness leads to success, but this is particularly true with ministry. The reason laziness is so destructive for ministry success is because progress isn't measured by productivity but rather by faithfulness to the person and work of Jesus Christ.

The call to serve God and others is an all-consuming lifestyle. Relationships can be both life-giving and life-draining. The duty of ministry often places us in highly draining situations. If our hearts seek leisure rather than service, we will experience frustration and burnout.

When my (Steve's) son was going through cancer treatments, there were days and nights I didn't think I would make it. Sleeping on a couch in the children's hospital so my wife could get rest in her own bed meant leaving the hospital early in the morning, driving an hour home to shower, and then heading into the office for a long day of meetings and ministry. Then, that night was back to the hospital. The months he spent in a hospital room were unbearable for him. And they were wearying for me. When people ask how my wife and I were able to survive those years, my response is always the same: "We didn't have a choice." Did we need rest? Of course. But did we endure for the sake of our son?

Without question. If we had been in love with leisure, we would have left him to suffer alone so we could play golf or take a beach trip or just take a nap at home away from the pain and suffering. But what kind of parent does that?

And the same thing is true with ministry. There are seasons when you will be tired, and you will think that you will not be able to make it. Obviously, those seasons cannot last forever. There will be moments when long-term survival requires you to rest. It is important to realize that rest and leisure are not the same thing. Your body needs rest. Your mind needs rest. Your soul needs rest in Christ. But an unwillingness to embrace hard times or hard work is a sign of selfishness and pride, not faithfulness to ministry. Finding the balance between laziness and much-needed rest can be difficult.

Laziness exhibits itself in avoidance. We avoid hard work, hard people, or hard situations because they make us uncomfortable. Rest is being comforted, not comfortable. As a minister, I may not be comfortable facing a difficult situation, but I am comforted knowing of God's faithful work within that situation. Laziness is looking to be comfortable rather than comforted. Neglecting hard and necessary work in favor of ease of life may last for a brief time, but ministry is not accomplished through avoiding difficult situations, but through leaning into those situations and applying the gospel of Jesus Christ to them. Lazy people rarely risk the hard work of ministering to people.

In ministry, laziness may cause us to avoid people we view as problems or situations that take time and creativity. It will also cause us to neglect the important, but not urgent, aspects of the job—sermon preparation, evangelism, equipping staff and lay-leaders, or even caring for those in our ministries who need us. Perhaps worst of all, laziness may also cause us to neglect our own spiritual development and growth.

Laziness leads to failure to faithfully walk with people in the work of the gospel. Building relationships with people, teaching them to follow Jesus, walking with them in times of hurt and pain, and all of the other aspects of ministry require us to be available for people. If we train ourselves to be passionate about leisure to the point of laziness, we may seek leisure as a means of avoiding people or a situation because they make us uncomfortable. We may end up neglecting people in order to indulge ourselves in leisure. Resisting the temptation to be lazy is vital for lasting ministry. Lazy ministers rarely see spiritual fruit.

Affection for Selfish Gratification

It really goes without saying that Christian ministers must avoid immorality. Of course, all Christians are called to avoid immorality. Selfish gratification is a character trait that goes far beyond immoral or unethical activity. Selfish ministers are certainly vulnerable to disqualifying and destructive sins, but they are likewise vulnerable to sinful actions towards others that prevent faithful ministry. A pastor who always has to "have his way" when it comes to decisions in the church will be a destructive presence in that church. Selfish gratification does not always have to be realized in immorality, it might also manifest itself in a leadership style that is manipulative or heavy-handed. Selfish people are hurtful people.

Ministry requires selflessness. A selfless character enables the ministry to take proactive steps to shun immorality. Rather than a self-indulgent attitude, those in ministry must follow the model of Phil 2:3–8, having the mind of Christ in which self-sacrifice for the spiritual well-being of others trumps any selfish indulgence. Resisting any affection for selfish gratification guards the minister from a lifestyle of treating others poorly for selfish gain.

Affection for Accolades

Ministers who pursue accolades and the applause of other people will ultimately fall short of God's design for ministers. An eighteenth-century Moravian missionary is reported to have told his students that their goal as missionaries was to "preach the gospel, die, and be forgotten." The point of this instruction was not that they should not leave behind a legacy of faithfulness that could be remembered, but that their goal in ministry was not to make a name for themselves. In Gen 11:4, God chastises the people building the Tower of Babel because they desired to make a name for themselves. Desire for accolades in ministry is embracing the spirit of Babylon. The better attitude is that of John the Baptist, who says of Jesus, "He must increase, but I must decrease" (John 3:30). Ministering with the character and mindset of John the Baptist is much preferable to that of the Babylonians! Rather than making a name for oneself, the faithful minister seeks to give glory and honor to the name of our God. Psalm 115:1 states this sentiment beautifully: "Not to us, Lord, not to us, but to your name give glory because of your faithful love, because of your truth."

As someone called to minister to others, you must beware the limelight because seeking a great name for yourself is incompatible with making disciples of Jesus. But on a practical level, seeking celebrity—even if that celebrity is just in your church—is an exercise in vanity. Virtually every star fades. Popular musicians, actors, and pop culture icons know that someone more talented, more attractive, or more seductive will come along to steal the spotlight. Celebrities have to become more outrageous to continue to be the center of attention.

Christian celebrities, like their cultural counterparts, typically do not handle diminished accolades with grace and kindness. As ministers who seek approval from others hear less applause, they are tempted to adjust their behavior to attract more attention. They hope people will like or at least appreciate them. Learning to resist the urge to seek the applause and approval of others is vital to faithful ministry. Pastors and other Christian leaders who cannot resist this urge will become worn out in pursuing accolades.

Affection for Wealth

Scripture warns us, "The love of money is a root of all kinds of evil, and by craving it, some have wandered away from the faith and pierced themselves with many griefs" (1 Tim 6:10). There is absolutely no place for an affection for wealth in the life of a minister. Loving the things of the world is incompatible with any Christian living, even more so for those seeking to lead men and women in following Jesus.

For the minister, one of the many dangers of loving money is becoming overwhelmed with "many griefs." When a pastor has an unhealthy affection for wealth, he may become envious of others who have more than he does. When a pastor begins to covet the wealth of others, he may become disenchanted with the church he is serving. He may even become disenchanted with the ministry altogether. In almost forty years of ministry, each of us has seen countless men and women leave assignments with churches in order to pursue more lucrative positions both in and outside of ministry.

One great challenge for ministers is that some churches—perhaps many—can be selfish toward their staff, using the calling of the minister as an excuse to underpay them. Far too many pastors have unnecessarily experienced poverty because of unkind churches. Scripture warns that someone who does not provide for their family is worse than an unbeliever (1 Tim 5:8). There is a balance between ministers needing to provide for their family and having an unhealthy love of money. Faithful ministry requires cultivating a heart of contentment when having less while also knowing what is needed to support a family. Paul models this heart when he writes, "I know how to make do with little, and I know how to make do with a lot. In any and all circumstances I have learned the secret of being content—whether well fed or hungry, whether in abundance or in need" (Phil 4:12). While most ministers will never be forced to go hungry, having a heart relentlessly devoted to Jesus rather than the pursuit of wealth is a necessary prerequisite to faithful ministry. Learning to love the things of God more than the things of the world will help the minister avoid all kinds of grief that results from discontentment and envy.

Each of these unhealthy affections contributes to an environment ripe for burnout. It takes a lot of work to pretend to be Christian. Pastors are tasked with not just helping other people grow into Christian maturity, but in modeling authentic Christian living for those in the congregation. Ministers are not super-Christians or even better Christians than everyone else in the church. Rather, they have the important role of teaching others to live Christianly while exemplifying what they teach. When pastors divorce their teaching from their conduct, they not only risk becoming exposed as hypocrites, but they burden themselves with the task of concealing their lack of integrity. Working hard to hide a character that is inconsistent with the message one is preaching can cause ministers to question their calling, to grow weary in the work, and to even begin to doubt the message they are preaching. Pastors have a duty to teach rightly and to live rightly. They must ensure that their conduct mirrors the message of the gospel and reflects a mature Christian character.

Cultivating Godly Character

In 1 Tim 3:1–7, Scripture sets a high standard of Christian character. All Christians are called to live godly lives. This call is even more important for those tasked with helping people in the church live up to this high standard of godliness. When outlining qualifications for those who oversee the ministry in the church, Paul says that they should be judged by a series of qualities and behaviors that exhibit spiritual maturity. Along with avoiding unhealthy affections, ministers must also cultivate healthy affections that are manifest in exemplary Christian behavior. And while the pressure to live an exemplary Christian life might be great, the consequences of failing to do so in ministry are even greater.

Cultivating a godly character is vital for the minister, first, because hypocrisy destroys trust and credibility. Trust is foundational in any relationship, and within the context of a congregation, it is paramount. A minister with a strong character builds trust and credibility, fostering a sense of security and authenticity among the church members. If people observe in their ministers a character that does not align with what they are being taught, they certainly are not going to have confidence in the message. Pastors can far too often be like parents with the attitude, "Do as I say, not as I do." The destructive nature of hypocrisy does not just damage the confidence church members have in their ministers, but it also damages their confidence in the gospel itself. Far too many people have walked away from church because of the failure of a pastor or other minister to live up to the message they are preaching.

Second, godly character also enables the minister to navigate challenges and controversies with wisdom and grace. Ministry is not immune to conflict, and how ministers handle adversity speaks volumes about their character. A minister of godly character faces difficulties with grace, humility, and perseverance. When facing personal trials, a minister can trust in the abiding presence of the Holy Spirit for strength and wisdom. A pastor who is walking with Jesus can better walk with a congregation through turbulent times. Ministers who cultivate a godly character are more dependable leaders during times of uncertainty because their confidence is not in themselves but in the wisdom and will of God.

Third, cultivating godly character impacts all the relationships a pastor experiences. Because the ministry is, fundamentally, building relationships for the purpose of spiritual formation, ministers need a character that facilitations godly relationships. Pastors are more than teachers on a stage. Their character must extend beyond the pulpit and into their personal lives. How many times has a pastor "fallen" because their true character came to light in their sinful behavior? Ministers struggle to be the same person among their family and friends as they are in their churches. This struggle can be mitigated by focusing on godly character as a prerequisite to godly behavior. How ministers live in their relationships demonstrates the authenticity of their character. Learning to be consistent in relationships with those in the church and outside of the church depends largely on the health of the minister's character.

Finally, formation of a godly character is the result of a commitment to continued maturity and spiritual growth. Ministers who refuse to mature are doomed to fail. You must cultivate a humble and teachable spirit, seeking feedback from others to help you address areas of weakness. There are blind spots in your own life with dangers that you may struggle to see. Godly men and women long for correction from those who can see the dangers in those blind spots. To effectively lead others in their spiritual growth, you have to be growing and maturing yourself.

Character for Faithful Ministry

It goes without saying that Christians in ministry are held to the highest moral and ethical standards. That is a given. But there are particular qualities of Christian character that are particularly applicable to ensuring an environment for healthy ministry and lifelong service to Christ and the church. While the "fruit of the Spirit" in Gal 5:22–23 is an excellent example of what a minister's life should reflect, there are a number of qualities anyone in ministry should cultivate to form the basis of fruitful ministry.

Humility

At the very core of Christian ministry is sacrifice and service. There is no room for pride and selfishness in ministry. To follow the example of Jesus in John 13:1–17, ministers must humble themselves both before God and before those whom they are called to serve. Pastors should recognize the threat of pride to the ministry of the gospel. Scripture chastises those ministers who put themselves and their preferences before the progress of the gospel. It has been said that "humility is not thinking less of yourself, but thinking of yourself less."[1] This is a good guide to cultivating a humble spirit. In many ways, humility can start with contrition over sin. When we remember that God has shown his love to us through Christ's death for sinners, we can emulate that sacrifice on behalf of others, whether they have "earned" sacrificial service or not. We best display the love of God

---

[1] Rick Warren, *The Purpose Driven Life: What on Earth Am I Here For?* (Grand Rapids: Zondervan, 2012), 149.

for us and for others when we exhibit selfless love for people in our care. This selfless love is not self-seeking or self-aggrandizing. Rather, it seeks out the best interests of others and treats them with grace and kindness. Humility keeps us from grasping after power, prestige, or prominence.

Love

Love certainly is a verb, but being a loving minister begins with a character that is loving. Developing a heart of genuine sympathy and compassion for people is essential to a lasting ministry. In Matt 9:36, we are told, "When he saw the crowds, he felt compassion for them, because they were distressed and dejected, like sheep without a shepherd." When ministers see troubled and helpless people and are not moved with compassion, they are not reflecting the character of Jesus. Dispassionate people cannot lead other people in following Jesus. Compassion for "sheep without a shepherd" is not mere sentimentalism. Christian compassion is recognition both of the great need of the person and the solution to that need. Every person is helpless in their sin. But the solution to their helpless state is the gospel of Jesus. A minister seeking to do gospel work without genuine love for people is creating the conditions for burnout because the underlying motivation for ministry to people is lost. Shepherds who have no concern for the sheep are like the Pharisees, who were passionate about their religious rules but lacked any compassion for people who were hurting and helpless. Ministers of all kinds, but particularly pastors, must cultivate a sense of love and compassion for all people.

Forgiveness

There is perhaps no more difficult character trait to develop than forgiveness. When we are offended by people, we do not naturally want to offer forgiveness. We much prefer justice to mercy, penance to pardon, and payment for any hurt we have suffered. But the Christian way of life is to forgive. In the Lord's Prayer, Jesus teaches us to pray, "Forgive us our sins, as we have forgiven those who sin against us" (Matt 6:12 NLT). Our own experience of God's forgiveness is rooted in being forgiving people. Paul instructs the church to forgive "one another, just as God also forgave you in Christ" (Eph 4:32). While all Christians are called to forgive, ministry is impossible without a forgiving spirit. Just as ministers must love people to minister effectively to them, ministers must also be quick to forgive people who offend them. Continuing the analogy from before, people, like sheep, can be difficult to lead. Despite the fact that you are seeking to lead people to a place of blessing, they may resist that leadership. They may knowingly or unknowingly hurt your feelings. People may question motives, spread rumors, and participate in gossip. There are innumerable ways you will suffer offense in the church. But if you are to not only survive ministry, but thrive in it, you must grow into a forgiving person.

There are two major reasons a lasting ministry requires you to have a forgiving spirit. First, the gospel demands that we forgive other people. Your message of forgiveness will fall on deaf ears if you do not practice it. Second, relationships require forgiveness. Every relationship you will ever be in will have some element of offense. That offense may be a great betrayal or a minor indiscretion, but there will be hurt. For the relationship to continue and be healthy, you will have to forgive the other person. If you cannot forgive, you cannot be in ministry.

A lack of forgiveness will plant the seeds of bitterness and you will find it more and more difficult to care for others if you are constantly thinking about the hurt and broken relationships caused by these hurts. This attitude will create a prison around your heart and will make it impossible to minister the love and grace of the Lord.

Patience

If forgiveness is the most difficult characteristic of the Christian life to practice, patience is a close second. But remaining in ministry requires patience as much as any other Christian virtue. Ministers must first be patient with *God*, learning to wait on his will. Trusting God means trusting his timing as well as his purposes. Second Peter addresses those who wonder why Jesus has not yet returned to end the injustice in the world, reminding them that God's purpose is to patiently wait so that others might come to repentance as well (2 Pet 3:9). If we can trust God's timing in the return of Christ, surely we can learn to trust his timing in our ministry!

Second, ministers must be patient with *people*. Life takes time. Ministry takes time. Disciples grow and mature over time, not in an instant. I think about being a parent. When our kids are learning to read or write or do math, we don't mock them or snatch the book away when they make a mistake. We know that growth requires patience even when the growth is slow and even frustrating. Imagine if we treated new disciples of Jesus in the same manner. When someone is born again, they become a child of God. They begin to crawl and walk and eventually run as disciples. Just as parenting takes considerable patience, so too does ministry. We have to learn to wait patiently on people to grow, walking alongside them through their failures and their successes (1 Thess 5:14), cheering them on to love and good works as we strive together for spiritual maturity (Heb 10:24–25). Impatient people will not make faithful or fruitful ministers.

Finally, we have to be patient with our *circumstances*. Life can be hard. We will face challenges and setbacks in our own growth. We will have failures. Ministers are not immune from suffering painful circumstances in life such as losing a job, receiving a tragic medical diagnosis, or watching a child walk away from the faith. Ministers must have a character that is capable of enduring difficulties in order to remain in the ministry to which they have been called. Cultivating that character trait is vital to endurance in ministry.

Discipline

Ministry does not simply happen on its own. Those called to ministry must learn to discipline themselves to fulfill the tasks associated with shepherding the souls of other people. A disciplined minister will show unwavering integrity, demonstrating honesty and a principled life. Discipline also entails a consistency in caring for others and fulfilling their work that is a model for others in the church. Disciplined ministers remain focused on the essential elements of Christian living and are not easily distracted from the mission. Part of developing a disciplined life is remembering that the purpose of ministry is to help people grow in their relationship with Jesus. Serving Jesus requires disciplined Christian living, disciplined personal lives, and disciplined ministry to others.

Conclusion

The purpose of this chapter is to serve as a reminder to heed the command from Scripture: "watch your life and doctrine closely" (1 Tim 4:16 NIV). The quickest way to undermine any ministry is to fall short of the character expected of those in ministry. Our goal is not to create extra pressure or to challenge you to live in a way that is entirely different than the life all Christians should be living. That is not to put undue pressure on ministers, as though the higher standard to which they are held is anything more than the standard all Christians are expected to attain. Instead, it is to remind you that your character is as much a part of your ministry as your teaching or your praying or your hospital visits or your small group facilitating.

The actions you perform as a minister are vehicles to help people grow in the same faith in which you are growing. The exhibition of God's gracious work in your life by means of his indwelling Spirit is a message and a motivation to those in your ministry. Without the foundational Christian character the Spirit produces, you are nothing more than an empty vessel. If you want to see fruit in your ministry, you must be a vessel that is set apart for God's use (2 Tim 2:21). If God has called you into the ministry to serve him and others, he has given you his Spirit to shape you into the man or woman he has designed you to be. Moreover, trying to serve Jesus without abiding in him will lead to frustration, failure, fruitlessness, and, ultimately, burnout.

{ CHAPTER 6 }

Workaholics Don't Die Winners; They Die Empty

"Come to me, all of you who are weary and burdened, and I will give you rest. Take my yoke upon you and learn from me, because I am lowly and humble in heart, and you will find rest for your souls. For my yoke is easy and my burden is light."

—Matt 11:28–30

Principle: The Sabbath was made for man, not man for the Sabbath.

Introduction

Imagine this scene.

A mass of people gathering around a covered figure. Torches cast a haze across the event. Drums stir the crowd, and they begin to dance and sway to the beat. On a platform in the middle of the ceremony, a figure pulls a rope, the cover drops, unveiling a massive statue. The leader raises his arms to silence the music and proclaims, "Behold your God. Serve him!"

Perhaps you remember a scene like this from movies like *Indiana Jones* or *King Kong*. Maybe you think about Shadrach, Meshach, and Abednego, or the golden calf that Aaron made for the Israelites while Moses received the law from God. Each of these stories tells the story of primitive idolatry. The scenes are a mixture of fear, joy, power, and dread.

We have traveled the world and have visited temples, holy sites, and other places of worship. While some travelers look at these places with a sense of wonder, as Christians and missionaries, we are constantly consumed by sadness. It's a reminder that millions of people continue to wander in darkness and hopelessness. The masses seek some form of redemption or restoration to a right relationship with the creator. But the way of idolatry is futile. It is a never-ending cycle of ritual and hand-wringing. The question always remains unanswered—Is it enough this time? Inevitably, the answer is no, so the ritual continues, and the gods remain unmoved.

Now, you might be asking yourself, This is an odd introduction. What in the world does idolatry have to do with ministry burnout?

We are glad you asked.

As we think about the subject of this book, we are convinced that this may be one of the more critical themes we discuss. You see, the painful reality is that many of us face burnout because we have shifted our focus from doing ministry as a partnership with God to serving ministry as if it were our god. In a word, we have made ministry an idol.

The words of Tim Keller are especially helpful. In the book *Counterfeit Gods,* he notes that an idol is, "anything that absorbs your heart and imagination. . . . An idol is whatever you look at and say, in your heart of hearts, 'If I have that, then I'll feel my life has meaning, then I'll know I have value, then I'll feel significant and secure.'"[1]

In our Western sophistication, we often reduce idolatry to the primitive scene we described above. However, this is just one type of idolatry. In its most basic form, idolatry is looking to a created thing as something worthy of worship. Shifting our devotion, identity, and hope from our creator to a lesser thing.

We all know that our primary duty is to worship God alone. Scripture is full of warnings against shifting our devotion from the one true God to anything of lesser value:

- The first two of the Ten Commandments forbid false worship and fashioning false gods.
- Moses regularly warned the Israelites of the dangers of worshiping the gods of other nations.
- Jeremiah mocks the nations for their foolishness, worshipping a god they had created with their own hands (See Jeremiah 10).
- In his letter to the Christians in Rome, Paul pointed out the wickedness of false worship as the beginning of more sinful behavior (See Romans 1).
- Then, in the final book of our Bible, John sees in the final judgment a connection between false worship and God's wrath.

---

[1] Timothy Keller, *Counterfeit Gods: The Empty Promise of Money, Sex, and Power, and the Only Hope That Matters* (New York: Penguin Random House, 2009), xix–xx.

Idolatry is a serious sin. In the Bible, those who are found guilty face severe punishment. At the same time, we can be sure that one reason Bible writers repeat this warning so often (and include many living examples) is that it is a temptation common to man. As we struggle with our own sense of sin and inadequacy, we look for something or someone to help. It is easier to "trust in" something we can see and predict rather than in a God we cannot see and who does not conform to our wishes.

Furthermore, those of us in ministry are not immune to this temptation. When we anchor our purpose, our identity, or our hope in the work or demonstrable results, we make ministry our master and our god. This is idolatry, and it is a sure path to burnout.

The idea that your approach to ministry may be idolatry is probably difficult to process. You work hard, and you also understand the consequences of doing the job well—people live and die without Christ. Also, you may wonder how you can do ministry for God and, at the same time, be guilty of misplaced worship. Perhaps it'll be more helpful to use a more modern term, one that feels less confrontational: we are *workaholics.*

Understand, we are not using this term as a description for someone who works hard or who finds themselves in seasons of imbalance or exhaustion. These moments are a normal part of any job. Long days, hurting people, and complicated ministry moments make our jobs hard. However, we use the label *workaholic* to highlight the unhealthy drive of many who engage in ministry as an addict. Just like a junkie or someone addicted to any other drug or feeling, a workaholic approaches ministry from an unhealthy need. The work becomes the source of hope, identity, devotion, and the reason for existence. Perhaps worse, some do ministry as the means for maintaining a right relationship with God, serving as a means of eliminating guilt or believing that the more successful we are, the more God approves of us. The sacrifices are viewed as meritorious—they make us more right with God. Then, just like the primitive idol we discussed earlier, we labor under the endless feeling of guilt, fear, and emptiness. Ministry is not God, and you cannot use it to save yourself.

In this chapter, we want you to remember this mathematical equation:

$$\text{Workaholism} = \text{Idolatry}$$
$$\text{Workaholism} \neq \text{Christian Ministry}$$

The premise is simple: Christian ministry is hard work. It is often unpredictable and demands seasons of imbalance and personal sacrifice. But it is not our reason for getting up each morning, and it should not be the primary source of ultimate identity. As Christians, we worship the Lord God, our creator, through Jesus. Gospel ministry is our partnership with him as he works in and through us to accomplish his will. This service may be a platform for worship, but we cease worshiping as Christians when our identity and hope rests on the stage of our work. Worship and work are not synonymous. In ministry, we submit to Christ's work and respond with our own worship of the one worthy of our love, devotion, and allegiance. We work in ministry in response to God's work in our own lives and serve others in order to bring glory to the One at work in Christ reconciling the world to himself.

Workaholism and Its Cure

It is not unusual for those involved in ministry to flirt with workaholism. In fact, this is one sin that our modern world encourages, even applauds. The frantic labor is often compared to laziness, and the response is something like, "I'd rather burn out than rust out." But remember, being a workaholic cannot be measured by the amount of work or the pace of work. Instead, it should be measured by our motivation and sense of hopelessness.

I have a friend named Todd who served as an Associational Mission Strategist. Part of his job consisted of encouraging and leading pastors in Northwest Florida to reach their communities. He also met regularly with these pastors for prayer and ministry. He tells me that through the years, he has observed that the most depressing day of the week for pastors was Monday. Every week, these men would gather, and conversations always opened with the question, "Whatcha run yesterday? How many did you have?" These always referenced attendance, offering, or some other quantitative measurement for success.

"The worst Monday of the year was the Monday after Easter," according to Todd. "Many of these brothers had hoped for high attendance and significant decisions for Christ, and when this didn't materialize, they were hopelessly depressed."

Rather than finding hope in the reality of the resurrection, these pastors were guilty of placing their identity and self-worth in the fickle response of sinful people. In some instances, they'd believed the lie that Sunday's attendance was a measure of God's favor or, worse, the means for earning his approval. This is the essence of idolatry. It also reveals the ugly reality of workaholism—addicted to the work, never satisfied, always chasing the next high.

As we confront this sin, we need to honestly look at Christian ministry to see if we can identify why leaders are tempted to workaholism and why we so quickly shift from serving the Lord through ministry to serving the ministry as our lord.

First, ministry is a sacred task. Whether you are a pastor, missionary, or serve in some other ministry role, your work deals with a holy and life-changing message. You handle the Word of God and dispense advice you believe conforms with his will. As a result, there is a real sense that you are standing in for the Lord. We often approach the work as if God is a boss who has stepped away for a moment and deputized us to take his place. The danger is that we begin to act as though our words are a replacement for his words or that our vision supplants God's vision for the ministry. If we are careless about our dependence on God, we can assume ownership of God's ministry to people, replacing his work with our own work.

I (Scott) remember being called upon to perform a funeral. I was a new pastor. The lady who died was a long-time member of the church. I didn't know her or her family, but I'd been told that none of her children ever attended church. With this in mind, my goal was to preach the gospel and win some to faith in Jesus.

On the night of the visitation, I mingled with the family and tried to give them some comfort. In the process, one of the daughters grabbed my hand and said, "Since you work for God and are close to him, if I touch you, it is like touching God." Of course, this wasn't true—but the sentiment remains. Any of us who have served in ministry for any period of time understand the unique pressure of being treated as if we were the Lord himself. The sacred aspects of ministry can become addictive or the source of our identity.

Second, the responsibilities we are entrusted with often require us to sacrifice personal time and a "normal" life. We enter into this life in obedience to God's calling. For this reason, we dare not take it lightly. The seriousness of the work can sometimes make it difficult to distinguish between the rigorous demands of the job and the will of God.

Christian ministry is a serious responsibility, and we can't minimize this truth. The Bible points out that the responsibility includes presenting everyone complete in Christ Jesus (Ephesians 4). And yet, there is a fine line between living a sacrificial life that places the needs of others above our own and assuming that our sacrifices are part of God's plan for salvation or sanctification. We treat ministry as an idol when we do the work as a means of grace.

And finally, the responsibilities in ministry often require hard work and long hours. We are pulled into people's lives at a moment of crisis and can't reasonably say "No" or "Not right now." This lifestyle can be physically and emotionally draining. However, it is also possible that we train our minds to live from one ministry "high" to another. Like an addict, we need a new "bump" to make us feel spiritually alive.

We are reminded of a story of a college student who was required to serve an internship with the local police station. Every day, her responsibility was to record the statistics and report crime numbers to those in leadership. Occasionally, she was invited to visit different crime scenes. One day, when she came home, her roommate asked about her day. "It was kinda boring. Nothing exciting happened."

"Isn't that a good thing?" The roommate asked. The response caught the student by surprise, but she had to admit that it was indeed good when she had less crime to report.

The adrenaline of ministry can be just as deceptive. It's not that we deal in the seedy elements of society, but we are tempted to confuse movement and activity with the work of God. Doing the work is the end goal. God, too often, is irrelevant and easily replaced by "the ministry."

Eugene Peterson warns pastors (and others involved in Christian ministry):

> We want gods that are not gods so we can "be as gods." . . . The idolatry to which pastors are conspicuously liable is not personal but vocational, the idolatry of a religious career that we can take charge of and manage . . . a call from God exchanged for an offer by the devil for work that can be measured and manipulated at the convenience of the worker.[2]

Perhaps the greatest danger here is that the results that accompany each of these impulses feel so right. These

---

[2] Eugene H. Peterson, *Under the Unpredictable Plant: An Exploration in Vocational Holiness* (Grand Rapids: Eerdmans, 1992), 4–5.

pressures develop habits of work that produce results. Many of those we labor alongside will be impressed and even offer genuine applause. But the goal of this chapter is to remind you that being a workaholic is not Christian; it is not healthy or helpful. It is a path away from God and toward burnout and disaster. You may be experiencing external results that garner the praise and respect of others. But you are becoming painfully aware that your heart has created an idol and your work is serving a false god.

Dealing with Workaholism

It may seem redundant, but it is worth repeating: the cure for workaholism and the idolatry of ministry (just like the cure for any sin) can be found in the Bible. Take a few moments and meditate on these words from Jesus:

> Come to me, all of you who are weary and burdened, and I will give you rest. Take my yoke upon you and learn from me, because I am lowly and humble in heart, and you will find rest for your souls. For my yoke is easy and my burden is light. (Matt 11:28–30)

To better understand this passage, it is important to consider its background. In this chapter, Matthew recounts several stories about Jesus's response to those struggling with unmet expectations and wavering faith. He is speaking to men and women who had their hope set on something that did not seem to be working out as they had anticipated.

The chapter opens with an uncomfortable scene. John the Baptist sends some of his disciples to ask Jesus about his true identity. These questions are even more shocking when we realize that just eight chapters before, John had declared his faith in Jesus as the Messiah. Remember the scene in Matthew 3 when John baptized Jesus? At that moment, he was so sure of Jesus's identity that he actually refused Jesus's request and instead asked to be baptized himself. Now John is in prison, and it appears that his confidence is fading. Some scholars have suggested that perhaps he is growing a bit impatient with the timing of Jesus's ministry.

With this as the backdrop, John's disciples approached Jesus with the question, "Are you the one who is to come, or should we expect someone else?" (Matt 11:3). John's frustration is easy to understand. His public and popular ministry had been interrupted. Now, he is asking himself if he had built his life on false hope. Had he misunderstood God's plan? It is not unusual for external pressures and events to cast a shadow of doubt over internal experiences.

This story is followed by Jesus's challenge to the religious leaders, men who also questioned his identity. They used his behavior—eating and drinking—as the indicator that he could not be the promised Messiah. In response, Jesus declared their lack of faith was worse than the sin of Tyre and Sidon and Sodom (Old Testament cities representing the pinnacle of rebellion).

In the face of these questions, Jesus calls on all who are struggling to come to him—bring your doubts, fears, questions, and concerns to the Savior. First, come and receive "rest." The word *rest* (Greek: *anapauō*) refers to finding relief from toil. In this context, this promise is specifically addressed to those whose exhaustion is related to the work they did to please God. Their frustration seemed to be the result of their seeking God's favor, a pursuit destined for failure and resulting in spiritual emptiness and exhaustion. Craig Blomberg notes, "The rest Jesus offers his disciples enables them to overcome a certain measure of 'fear, anxiety, uncertainty, and meaninglessness in the joy and peace of God's very presence in Jesus Christ'"[3] It is an invitation to cease striving because Jesus is what you have been seeking.

Second, Jesus invites those who are tired of carrying these burdens to stay with him, to lay down their self-imposed burdens and join the work alongside Jesus. Labor is no longer a burden as we learn to labor alongside Jesus; we serve in his strength. Our work is not our identity or hope. On the contrary, it is in the midst of this work one finds genuine soul rest. Have you allowed ministry to become your idol? Do you find yourself frustrated, wondering if you have placed your hope in the wrong place? If so, Jesus's invitation is for you.

Sabbath as a Day and a Person

Perhaps one of the first steps toward addressing the idolatry of being a workaholic is to embrace the central biblical truth of Sabbath. Even a quick reading of the Bible shows this is an important theme. The idea of Sabbath is presented as part of the creation story, and it is continued through into the Ten Commandments. God called the Israelites, attention to his working and resting and then instituted the Sabbath as part of their rhythm of life.

---

[3] Craig L. Blomberg, *Matthew*, New American Commentary, vol. 22 (Nashville: Broadman & Holman, 1992), 194.

In the New Testament, we find examples of abusive teaching about the Sabbath, but Jesus doesn't completely dismiss the idea. Instead, he says that the Sabbath was created for man. It is God's plan for a healthy lifestyle that accepts both our human frailty and our need for God. God created men and women in his image, but we are also human beings; we are not divine.

Furthermore, in a fuller and greater sense, this understanding of Sabbath as a day is a sign of God's covenant and a foretaste of his eternal rest, which is found in Christ, who is our rest. With this in mind, we need to remind ourselves that Sabbath is also a person—Jesus. He is our rest. This is what the writer of Hebrews has in mind with the words:

- "For we who have believed enter the rest" (Heb 4:3).
- "Therefore, a Sabbath rest remains for God's people. For the person who has entered his rest has rested from his own works, just as God did from his. Let us, then, make every effort to enter that rest, so that no one will fall into the same pattern of disobedience" (Heb 4:9–11).

Ray Stedman notes the promises found in these verses "makes clear that truly keeping the Sabbath is not observing a special day . . . but sabbath keeping is achieved when the heart rests on the great promise of God. . . . *We cease from our own works* and look to his working within us to achieve the results that please him."[4] Christ himself is our rest because it is in him that we cease striving to please God. In his

---

[4] Ray C. Stedman, *Hebrews,* IVP New Testament Commentary Series (Downers Grove: IVP Academic, 1992), 58–59.

atonement and resurrection, Jesus took the penalty, shame, guilt, and final punishment for our sin. By faith, we are declared right with God, and there is nothing we can do to make him think better or worse of us. According to 2 Cor 5:21, in Christ, we *are* the righteousness of God.

When we grasp the truth of Sabbath as a day and a person, the unhealthy addiction and idolatry of ministry vanishes. When our ministries consist of nonstop labor and endless pursuit of unhealthy worship, we dishonor God's name, and we miss out on the blessings that he has prepared for us. Though it may feel rewarding and right to engage in ministry as a workaholic, this is not of the Lord. It is also a sure path to burnout.

God created us in his image, and our work can glorify him and serve others. However, this work (even work that is ministry) is not the purpose or goal of our lives. Work is meant to be balanced with rest, worship, and relationships. Being excessively devoted is not the Christ-honoring lifestyle that a minister should pursue.

Practical Steps for Addressing Idolatry

When we think about overcoming the idolatry that is workaholism, one passage of Scripture comes to mind: Jesus's words to the Ephesian church in the book of Revelation.

> I know your works, your labor, and your endurance, and that you cannot tolerate evil people. You have tested those who call themselves apostles and are not, and you have found them to be liars. I know that you have persevered and endured hardships

> for the sake of my name, and you have not grown weary. But I have this against you: You have abandoned the love you had at first. Remember then how far you have fallen; repent, and do the works you did at first. Otherwise, I will come to you and remove your lampstand from its place, unless you repent. (Rev 2:2–5)

Though this passage is addressed to a specific church, the message is perfect for someone who has traded serving the Lord through ministry to serving ministry as a god.

First, this passage reminds the reader that productivity is not the same as loving Jesus. This letter describes several admirable ministry metrics. The church approached the ministry with enthusiasm and endurance. They seemed to value sound doctrine and even be willing to confront heresies with the real gospel. However, despite these accolades, Jesus says that this church is not in love with him. According to Michael Wilcock, this accusation singles out "the one quality without which all others are worthless."[5] When ministry is reduced to activity and productivity, it is unpleasing to our Lord.

Loveless ministry is an apt description of workaholism because, as one practices the work, neither the Lord nor the people whom we serve are the intended goal. Instead, the end goal is ministry itself—how much can be done, how efficiently it can be achieved, and how much credit can be

---

[5] Michael Wilcock, *The Message of Revelation: I Saw Heaven Opened*, rev. ed., The Bible Speaks Today (Downers Grove: IVP Academic, 2021), 20.

passed around. It is important to observe that, of the seven letters written to the churches in Revelation, this is the only church that Jesus threatens with extinction: "I will come to you and remove your lampstand from its place, unless you repent" (Rev 2:5). When ministry becomes an idol, Jesus is under no obligation to sustain it; in fact, he may stand in opposition to it.

Thankfully, this letter does not proceed directly from judgment to destruction. God is gracious, and he provides a way back. If you have seen yourself in the description of ministry idolatry presented in this chapter, keep reading. In the story of the lost son, once the prodigal starts home, the father was waiting to welcome him back. Similarly, the path back is open, and your heavenly Father is waiting.

The way home is provided in verse 5: "Remember then how far you have fallen; repent, and do the works you did at first" (Rev 2:5). As followers of Jesus Christ, we have turned our attention to him as our Lord. And when we find that our attention has been drawn away, we repent and renew our worship of him alone.

Look Back

Jesus tells this church that the first step away from this idolatry is to remember where things started and recognize your fall. Suppose we consider again Jesus's story of the lost son in Luke 15. His decisions, coupled with several unfortunate circumstances, left him in a desperate situation. In fact, Jesus says that he was so far gone that he wanted to eat the pigs' food. But the first step out of the pig pen was looking back, remembering life before. With this, he reminded himself of the benefits of living back at home. This memory provided the motivation and hope for the next step.

In Chapter 2, we explored the reality of God's call to ministry. This divine call was the result of several important circumstances coming together in your life. Though each of us indeed experienced God's call differently, can you remember that moment when you knew God's hand was guiding your thoughts and the circumstances around you towards ministry? Most of us approached that moment with a sense of humility and even dread. I (Scott) remember praying, "God, if you can do anything with me, I'm yours." And the important part of this little prayer was that I meant it. Now, years later, with decades of experience and training, it is often necessary to revisit that moment as a reminder that it should always be about what God will do.

For the church in Ephesus, Jesus did not command them to look around at all the good happening in their ministry. He pointed back to a time when they served him out of love. It is pretty telling to note that even though Jesus can point to a list of important ministry accomplishments, they are all part of the fall. You may be doing a lot. It may seem that the Lord is blessing the work, but is the productivity and the work part of your falling into idolatry?

Pause long enough to look back and remember where you have fallen from.

Look Up

The only proper response to our awareness of sin is to repent. This pattern can be seen in many different places in the Bible. Looking again at the parable of the lost son, we find this speech, "Father, I've sinned against heaven and in your sight" (Luke 15:21). We see a similar response from the pen of King David after the prophet confronted him of his sin, "Against you—you alone—I have sinned and done this evil in your sight" (Ps 51:4). It should come as no surprise that Jesus's command for the church in Revelation 2 to look back and remember is followed by a stern call to repent.

There is much confusion about the meaning of repentance today. For some, repentance is simply an acknowledgment of wrongdoing. For others, repentance is understood as signaling sorrow or regret. While it is true that genuine repentance will include each of these phases, sincere repentance is much more. According to Grant Osborne, the word used here that we translate into English as *repent* refers to "a change of heart, involving repudiation of the past as well as an embrace of a new lifestyle."[6] In other words, repentance may begin with emotion and regret (2 Cor 7:10), but it is measured as genuine when these emotions lead to a changed life—a new life.

Looking back leads to conviction and reveals where things have gone wrong. Looking up draws us away from current circumstances and into the presence of God. It may be true that your workaholism has wounded your family, your church, your friends, and others. It is also true that repentance will include apologies and rebuilding these relationships. However, as we have argued through this chapter,

---

[6] Grant R. Osborne, *Revelation*, Baker Exegetical Commentary on the New Testament (Grand Rapids: Baker Academic, 2002), 117.

at its heart, workaholism is idolatry. It is serving ministry as a god. For this reason, we need to take this to the Lord himself. Confess it as a sin and ask him to remind you that at the heart of the matter, you have substituted the worship of God for worshiping a man-made ministry.

The good news is that repentance may begin with tears and shame, but it is the pathway to restoration. I remember several years ago reading through the book of Jonah and being shocked by his complaint against God. Apparently, the prophet couldn't stand the idea of his enemies being forgiven, and so he didn't want to preach to them. He knew God's character and realized that if the people of Nineveh would repent, God would forgive them: "I knew that you are a gracious and compassionate God, slow to anger, abounding in faithful love, and one who relents from sending disaster" (Jonah 4:2).

Brothers and sisters, behold your God!

Look Ahead

Finally, Jesus tells this church to get back to work again but to do the first works. In this case, repentance should be understood as turning back to the Lord, but also as turning away from work done the wrong way to do the old work well.

Throughout this chapter, we have continually reminded ourselves that Christian ministry is hard work. It is a mistake to equate *workaholism* with working hard. This final, practical step for renewed ministry is to do the work but with a new vision and a new hope. No longer is our ministry the source of happiness and joy. We refuse to measure God's love for us or our love for him on the responses of fickle and sinful people. The first work is a work of love and worship of the Lord.

This chapter is a call to a new day. It is a challenge to break away from business as usual and refuse to join the masses who are giving their soul to their work. God's primary call on your life was a call to himself. Your call to ministry is his means of making you into the man or woman he wants you to be. However, our materialistic culture produces a siren call to twist these callings. This is the short path to burnout because, while the ministry is a wonderful life, it is a terrible god. Like Shadrach, Meshach, and Abednego in Daniel 3, refuse to bow to this god. Maybe it is scary to think about the expectations of others, but remember the words of these three young men:

> Our God whom we serve is able to deliver us from the burning fiery furnace, and he will deliver us out of your hand, O king. But if not, be it known to you, O king, that we will not serve your gods. (Dan 3:17–18, ESV)

{ CHAPTER 7 }

Ministry in Community

Brothers and sisters, if someone is overtaken in any wrongdoing, you who are spiritual, restore such a person with a gentle spirit, watching out for yourselves so that you also won't be tempted. Carry one another's burdens; in this way you will fulfill the law of Christ.

—Gal 6:1–2

Principle: Leadership is a lonely path, but you were never intended to do it alone.

Everybody needs a friend like Samwise Gamgee.

Remember the scene in *The Lord of the Rings*? (If you haven't watched the movie or read the books, this paragraph is a bit of a spoiler, but they've been out long enough that it's on you.) Frodo Baggins is responsible for destroying the ring and saving the world from evil. At the climax of the saga, his strength fails as Frodo climbs the mountain to destroy the ring. He's wounded, tired, and ready to give up. The weight of his responsibilities and the physical toll of the journey have left him empty on the side of a jagged mountain. He is ready to give up.

Then, his faithful friend Sam leans into the moment. He reminds him of the importance of the task. He asks him, "Do you remember the Shire? Do you remember the taste of strawberries?" Each of these questions plays on memory and appeals to hope and motivation. When Frodo mumbles that he doesn't remember these things, Sam steps up, and in an ultimate show of friendship, he says of the ring and the task, "I can't carry it for you, but I can carry you." Then, he lifts Frodo and carries him through the completion of the mission.

This moment reflects the experience of our lives. In a very real sense, Christian ministry is a battle to overcome the consequences of sin (the ring) and give hope to those who have none. Like Frodo, you may have undertaken the journey with anticipation of greatness, but along the way, this journey has taken its toll.

- Maybe you are tired and beaten down.
- Maybe you are drawn toward the exact temptations you warn others to avoid.
- Perhaps you have forgotten the hope and can't remember the taste of strawberries.

You need friends—someone to keep you moving forward, reminding you of the reason for the struggle. Doing ministry alone takes its toll on your emotions and even your soul. We all need partners for the journey. And, if necessary, you'll have someone who will carry you for a little while when your strength fails.

Maybe the description above describes your current situation. Perhaps you are not yet in a season of exhaustion, but you sense it's just over the next hill—after the next event, sermon, or counseling session. Ministry is exhausting, but far too many find themselves alone in the journey. This chapter will serve to highlight the necessity of community and fellowship in ministry. As Ecclesiastes reminds us, "Pity the one who falls without another to lift him up" (Eccl 4:10). Pursuing ministry without authentic Christian community is a recipe for burnout.

In a survey conducted by Lifeway Research, 69 percent of pastors said that one of their greatest personal struggles was "friendships and fellowship with others." We believe it is safe to assume that those in other Christian ministries would similarly reflect the loneliness experienced by the pastors who responded to this survey. This means that the overwhelming majority of men and women serving in ministry are like Frodo, carrying the weight of the world but doing so without Samwise Gamgee at their side. Loneliness is an epidemic that leaves the minister vulnerable to burnout. However, the reverse would also be true. Doing ministry with partners in the work can make the load lighter, the journey more enjoyable, and the difficulties easier to bear.

Ministry Can Be a Lonely Life

Why is ministry such a lonely path? Our work is with people; we are quite literally surrounded by them all the time. Most of us must be creative to make enough time alone to study, think, write, and plan. Despite this, Christian ministry consists of some unique realities that make it more difficult to maintain meaningful friendships.

First, the nature of our work means that people are afraid they cannot be themselves around us. Pastors and others who are involved in full-time ministry seem to represent a value system many simply do not want to deal with because they may feel guilty. How often have you been in a situation where, after you introduced yourself and what you did for a living, you experienced an immediate shift in the tone of the conversation? All hope of regular interaction evaporates.

I (Scott) remember a time I played in a golf tournament. I was paired with a guy I hadn't previously known. We drove different carts, so after a brief introduction, we didn't engage in much personal talk during the match. But when we'd finished and stood around watching scores post, he asked me what I did for a living. When I told him I worked in a church, he got angry. He said it wasn't fair to keep that a secret because he would have behaved differently if he had known I was a pastor. He proceeded to apologize for his language and behavior on the course. Until that moment, we'd been regular guys playing golf together; I hadn't been offended by his language or behavior. However, when he learned I was in Christian ministry, everything changed. It was as if my job placed a magnifying glass over the last four hours of our life, and he felt judged. Real friendships require a degree of vulnerability and honesty that many are simply unwilling to pursue with a person in professional ministry.

Second, because ministry involves counseling, praying, teaching, and spiritual guidance, ministers often know intimate and uncomfortable details about others. One of the privileges of ministry is watching the hope of the gospel light up the dark crevasses of life; however, this also means that the time we spend with others is in a moment they would prefer to forget. When we offer counsel for a broken marriage or prayer for a wandering child, people share details of their lives that may later be something they'd prefer to forget.

Try as they might, sometimes others simply cannot disassociate the minister from the crisis moment they wish had never happened. The pastor was there when a loved one passed. The student minister knows the sins of teenagers. This feeling of distance does not allow for the type of interpersonal relationship necessary for deep and enduring friendships.

Another reason ministers struggle with friendships is because we are afraid of the responses or judgments of others. We struggle with insecurity or fear of being accused of favoritism, so ministers often keep others at arm's length. The weight of the daily grind contributes to relational exhaustion that erodes willingness to invest effort into building friendships. Isolation feels easier than risking criticism that is likely to come.

Despite these realities, living isolated, without at least a few deep friendships, is not brave or godly. It leaves a minister vulnerable to sin, attack, narrow thinking, and burnout. Deep friendships are not optional; they are essential. The need for genuine, growing friendships is not a sign of weakness or failure; these relationships are the source of strength and crucial to success. We should intentionally cultivate deep friendships to avoid burnout in all its forms.

The image of a solitary leader shouldn't be seen as a sign of spiritual maturity. Remember, Jesus called his disciples friends. If the Lord of the universe chose to relate to his followers in this way, why would we think we should be any different?

Consider these Proverbs about the importance of friendship:

- "A friend loves at all times, and a brother is born for a difficult time" (Prov 17:17).
- "The wounds of a friend are trustworthy, but the kisses of an enemy are excessive" (Prov 27:6).
- "Oil and incense bring joy to the heart, and the sweetness of a friend is better than self-counsel. Don't abandon your friend or your father's friend, and don't go to your brother's house in your time of calamity; better a neighbor nearby than a brother far away" (Prov 27:9–10).

The fictional friendship between Frodo and Samwise reverberates with us because of the way it affirms the biblical vision of Christian fellowship found in Gal 6:1–2:

> If someone is overtaken in any wrongdoing, you who are spiritual, restore such a person with a gentle spirit, watching out for yourselves so that you also won't be tempted. Carry one another's burdens; in this way you will fulfill the law of Christ.

Many consider the book of Galatians to be one of the harshest letters in the New Testament. Bible scholars have observed that in other letters Paul followed a formula in the opening salutation of his letters. This traditional structure included Paul's self-identification, identification of the letter's recipients, along with some type of thanksgiving or reflection on the relationship between the writer and reader. However, in this letter, the apostle skips the traditional "thanksgiving." Timothy George has observed, "Just where we would expect to find such a word of blessing and affirmation, Paul lashed out with his statement of astonishment concerning the apostasy of the Galatians, 'I am astonished that you are so quickly deserting' (1:6). In this way we are prepared for the tremendous emotional intensity of the letter that follows."[1] This same sharp tone continues throughout the rest of this letter.

This is one reason why the opening verses of chapter 6 jump out to the reader. A letter that strikes such a tone ends with a description of Christian love and support. Earlier in the letter, Paul uses phrases like "You foolish Galatians" and "Let them be accursed" in reference to those who succumbed to temptation (see Gal 3:1 and 1:8). Here, however, he implores other Christians to restore the offending brother and to join him in his fight, carrying the load of life together. Timothy George reminds us, "The church of Jesus Christ is not a charitable organization . . . It is rather a family of born-again brothers and sisters supernaturally knit together by the Holy Spirit in a common fellowship of mutual edification and love."[2] Even those of us who lead in the church are no less in need of support and edification than those we have been charged to care for.

This description of Christian friendship and support is built on several assumptions. As we unpack each, we remind

---

[1] Timothy George, *Galatians*, Christian Standard Commentary (Nashville: B&H, 2020), 460.

[2] George, 75.

ourselves why maintaining strong friendships is necessary for long-term survival in Christian ministry.

1. Because of the nature of this fallen world, we all face temptations and have to carry burdens that seem too great.

God created a perfect world and declared it "very good." However, we no longer live in that "very good" world. As Adam and Eve broke God's command, everything was turned upside down. Not only did their sin bring death and separation into the world, but it also introduced the harsh consequences of sin and rebellion. In the Lord's Prayer, Jesus instructs us to pray: "Your will be done on earth as it is in heaven" (Matt 6:10). This is a powerful prayer, but it is also a reminder that our world is not working the way God intended. The Bible is filled with an eschatological hope that God will one day restore what is broken; a day is coming when, in the words of our friend Samwise Gamgee, "Every sad thing will come untrue." But that day isn't today. We don't live in the new kingdom. Instead, according to Jesus's description of our lives today, "In this world you will have trouble" (John 16:33 NIV).

What are the consequences of living in a broken world?

First, temptation is ever present. According to the book of James, "Each person is tempted when he is drawn away and enticed by his own evil desire. Then after desire has conceived, it gives birth to sin, and when sin is fully grown, it gives birth to death" (Jas 1:14–15).

Can you see this progression? We all live in a world filled with opportunities to sin. As Christians, we have the freedom to choose not to sin (Romans 6). At the same time, we have a propensity to sin—desires that may be normal become "evil" when they consume our thinking and pull us into godless ways of fulfillment.

When I read this passage, I think about fishing. The fisherman devises a bait that takes advantage of the fish's natural desires—the desire for food, the desire to protect its territory, or the genuine curiosity of something strange in its world. The fish is "drawn away and enticed," then the hook is set, and the fish is now fighting for his life.

Brothers and sisters, just because you are in Christian ministry does not eliminate the temptations resulting from living in this fallen world. We all struggle under the weight of temptation and sin: lust, pride, greed, anger, selfishness, and the list could go on. While it is true that our work involves regular interaction with the things of God—preaching the gospel, teaching his truth, leading the church, and reaching the lost—it also includes criticism, rejection, and spiritual warfare. All of these can make us especially vulnerable to sin and temptation. Our ministry does not isolate us from temptations; in some ways, it makes us more vulnerable. This is why we cannot go at it alone.

2. Because God created us to live as part of a community, we make a grave mistake when we assume we should bear these burdens alone.

Our American culture has created an idol of the solitary hero who stands alone in the face of opposition. The *Dark Knight* operates alone, behind a mask, the singular hero that Gotham needs. He single-handedly rights the wrongs and punishes the bad guys. He appears seemingly out of nowhere, executes justice, then disappears into thin air. Most other superheroes are likewise solitary. These characters may make fine entertainment, but they are lousy models for ministry.

Some of us mistakenly believe we have to be strong and self-sufficient; we think we need to hide our weaknesses and struggles, appearing perfect and problem-free. These assumptions are not only wrong, they are also dangerous. They can lead to isolation, loneliness, depression, burnout, or even moral failure. No minister can survive or thrive in ministry alone. We need support, encouragement, accountability, and prayer from a growing relationship with others.

The Bible contains stories of friendships as essential components of leadership and ministry. We can think about David and Jonathan or Paul and his missionary team members. On the other end of the spectrum, we cannot forget the opening sentences of 2 Samuel 11.

> In the spring when kings march out to war, David sent Joab with his officers and all Israel. They destroyed the Ammonites and besieged Rabbah, but David remained in Jerusalem. One evening David got up from his bed and strolled around on the roof of the palace. From the roof he saw a woman bathing—a very beautiful woman. (2 Sam 11:1–2)

The writer of this passage is very clear: David's isolation left him vulnerable to temptation, and his lack of accountability opened the door for the sin that destroyed his ministry.

Another biblical example that demonstrates the necessity of supporting relationships in ministry is found in Exodus 18. The leadership role God gave Moses overwhelms him. According to the text, Moses spent all day listening to the people's problems. Neither Moses nor the people were being served. Then, Moses's father-in-law said, "What you're doing is not good. . . . You will certainly wear out both yourself and these people who are with you, because the task is too heavy for you. You can't do it alone" (Exod 18:17–18).

There are two key phrases in this passage; let's take them in reverse order.

First, *you cannot do it alone.*

The ministry challenge (the minister's life and ministry practice) cannot be accomplished alone. To be sure, there are moments when one is called upon to take a stand or do work that no one else is willing or capable of doing. However, even a casual reading of the Bible reminds us that loneliness has never been part of God's plan. Jethro's words are more than a statement about Moses's ability to accomplish the task (though that is undoubtedly true). It is also a caution about longevity and his own health.

Second, *what you are doing is not good.*

We don't know anyone who gets involved in Christian ministry to do bad things. It is possible there are charlatans and wicked people who do so, but we don't know any of them. Everyone we know, even those who end up doing wrong in ministry, wants to do good. This desire for good is also what drives many of us into isolation in ministry. "After all," we say to ourselves, "if you want something done right, you need to do it yourself."

However, according to Jethro's wise advice, this is not good. The same word is used to describe the creation when God said, "It is not good for the man to be alone" (Gen 2:18). It is used in other places to highlight beauty, desirability, and morality.

When we seek to do ministry and life alone, not only is this a recipe for lack of productivity and frustration, but it is also wrong. It is not how God intended us to live.

3. It is God's will that Christians walk alongside one another—we need others, and they need us.

It is not insignificant that Paul supports his command with the phrase, "In this way you will fulfill the law of Christ" (Gal 6:2). This clearly refers to Jesus's teaching, "I give you a new command: Love one another. Just as I have loved you, you are also to love one another. By this everyone will know that you are my disciples, if you love one another" (John 13:34–35). This phrase reminds us that relationships are not simply practical; they are part of what it means to live a Christian life.

Timothy George notes:

> As the Roman philosopher Seneca put it, "The primary sign of a well-ordered mind is a man's ability to remain in one place and linger in his own company." But there is a vast difference between Stoic equanimity and Christian courage. The myth of self-sufficiency is not a mark of bravery but rather a sign of pride.[3]

---

[3] George, *Galatians*, 461.

God's design for his children is life in community. The fact that ministry presents unique pressures, making relationships more complicated, does not render the law of Christ irrelevant. Just the opposite, we know that the law represents God's goodness and grace. God does not want ministers to bear their burdens alone or to ignore the burdens of others. He wants them to share their burdens. Doing so fulfills the law of Christ. It is his will, and it is for our good.

We hope you can find supportive relationships within your ministry—church members, staff, or other leaders. But we know that this isn't always possible. For some, it may be better for you to pursue meaningful friendships with other ministers in your area or friends you met at a conference or in seminary. These men and women will understand the complexities of ministry and your unique pressures. You can carry one another's burdens and even work to restore each other gently if you give in to temptation.

Practical Guidelines On Friendship

1. Be the friend you want others to be.

The language of Prov 18:24 has always echoed in our minds: "A man who has friends must himself be friendly" (NKJV). Being critical of others who aren't friendly to us is easy. But this verse reminds us that relationship responsibility also falls to us. Do you remember the Golden Rule? The principle is quite profound. Decide how you want others to treat you, and treat them that way (Matt 7:12).

There is probably no other context where this truth is more applicable than as it relates to relationships.

- Want a friend who will text you when you are down? Text them first.
- Want someone to remember your birthday? Remember their birthday.
- Want a friend who will pray for you and encourage you to godliness? Who are you praying for?
- Do you need someone willing to enter your chaos and help you with life? Walk into their chaos first.

If these principles seem simple, it is because they are. But we all know it is easier to criticize what others are not doing than to do for others as we want them to do for us.

2. Pray for other pastors.

Ask how you can pray for other ministry leaders and then actually pray. We all know the encouragement we feel when we share a burden and, later, someone asks about it. They let us know they have been praying. Be that friend for others, and others will be that friend for you.

When I (Scott) served overseas, one of my wife's missionary strategies was prayer. Anytime someone shared a need, she jotted it down and included it in her daily prayer routine. But she also took it one step further. Each time she saw that person, she told them she'd been praying and asked for an update. Over the years, this practice has provided the foundation for spiritual friendships.

3. Put yourself in places to meet others.

Building relationships takes time and effort; it rarely happens by accident. For this reason, you need to prioritize spending time with others and getting to know them personally. Don't just "talk shop."

Christian ministry can be a lonely island. We are around people, but they are the same people. Many only come to us when in need and then return to their everyday lives. If you want to develop more meaningful friendships, it may require you to do some things differently.

- *Attend a local ministers gathering.* Most cities have regular meetings designed for encouragement and fellowship. Perhaps your denomination sponsors such an event; if not, check around or start one in the area. When I (Scott) served as a pastor in a small town in Alabama, I met regularly with a group of pastors. Most of us were not from the same denomination; our doctrine didn't always align. But these men became a helpful group for prayer, shared ministry, and even advice over the years.
- *Participate in community events.* Join in with the city parade or other celebrations. If your kids play sports, don't just attend the games; consider coaching the team. Steve coached little league baseball/softball and football for his kids. It is not unusual for us to be out and be interrupted by someone who wants to talk to "Coach Mac."
- *Reach back in your past.* Don't let the tendency of mobility break the friendships you have worked to form. Some of our best friends are guys we attended seminary with or served with previously in different cities. Technology makes it easy to maintain

these friendships, and we need them for survival. Stay connected.

4. Be open and vulnerable.

Vulnerability is vital to building meaningful friendships. Share your struggles, fears, and doubts with others. Pastors, be yourself. Don't try to be someone you're not. This will help you build trust and deepen your relationships.

We realize vulnerability can be risky, and it is important to use wisdom and caution so you do not accidentally create stumbling blocks of ministry. God has placed us in the position of spiritual leadership, and this role requires a degree of discretion. However, genuine friendships require transparency. We hope you can find a couple of people you can rely on to carry your burdens and help as you confront sin and temptation.

5. Be patient

The friendships we write about in this chapter do not form overnight. As believers in Jesus, we have a common foundation; as Christian ministers, we share a common vision and direction. However, we cannot expect to become immediate confidants overnight.

For some, you may have bought into the lie that your ministry requires isolation. You may be out of practice or have created a lifestyle of loneliness. Before you see real progress, you will need to make changes. Be patient with yourself and others. The risk has a reward, even if the journey is uncomfortable.

A Personal Word

This book is not an academic exploration; it is a reflection of the many years we have been friends. It represents our seasons of ministry success as well as shared heartbreak. We are not simply co-authors of this book but also genuine friends. In fact, we have been friends longer than we have been married. We joke that we will always remain friends because we know too many secrets.

Through the years, we have watched men and women start a ministry with great intentions, only to burn out or flame out. The ministry that started with such promise ended in shame and disaster. When we thought about how to avoid this disaster, we shaped the book's outline. We thought about the things we'd learned through the years. However, after thinking about the other topics, we both agree that one of the best preventions against ministry burnout is the type of friendship we discuss in this chapter.

Our friendship has been forged in more than time. It has been our support through the most complicated, joyful, and sorrowful seasons of life (some of which you have read about in this book). We have served alongside each other in ministry, not always in the same cities or even the same countries. But always as unwavering support.

When we write about the dangers of loneliness and isolation, we do so from a genuine understanding of the importance of having others keep you grounded and sane when life is spinning out of control. We know what it means to live with an empty tank and realize we can look to someone else for support.

One time, Steve was in the middle of a sermon when a coughing fit hit. He tried to work through it but couldn't stop. The solution? He pointed to Scott to step up and finish the sermon. On another occasion, word came that Scott's mom was at the point of death. The first knock on the door was Steve and another friend named Greg. Together, they covered the rest of the week, which allowed Scott's family to travel while friends picked up the slack and kept ministry responsibilities flowing.

In seasons of doubt, frustration, sickness, and danger, as well as moments of great fun, excitement, and the awe-inspiring wonder of what Stephen Curtis Chapman once called "The Great Adventure," we have learned the value of partnership and friendship as protection from burnout.

We don't assume that every reader will have a lifelong relationship that lasts over half your life. However, it is our sincere prayer that this brief testimony will motivate you to begin asking God for a similar blessing. In this life, we will all have trouble. But by God's grace, we are not required to endure it alone.

{ CHAPTER 8 }

The People Are the Ministry

> Now there are different gifts, but the same Spirit. There are different ministries, but the same Lord. And there are different activities, but the same God works all of them in each person. A manifestation of the Spirit is given to each person for the common good.
>
> —1 Cor 12:4–7

Principle: Ministry is about people, be honest about your humanity.

Introduction

An unfortunate running joke among ministers is that "ministry would be great if it weren't for the people." On the one hand, this is a funny reference to the complexity of working with the demands and problems people bring to us. People in churches bring complex problems, long-held preferences, and even trauma with them into Christian relationships. Pastors spend their time seeking to minister to, and sometimes working to make happy, a wide variety of people.

At the same time, this joke can also betray an attitude that interprets ministry as a series of events or activities rather than an opportunity to fulfill Jesus's commission to "feed his sheep." Seeing ministry as consisting of the three Bs—bodies, budgets, and buildings—leads to frustration. When our vision for ministry is tainted, we are tempted to view the people with whom we minister as an obstacle to success. We must choose to view the people we serve as the true measure of success of our ministry rather than a hindrance. Learning to see people not as the means to an end, but as the proper end in itself, keeps us properly focused and prevents burnout.

As in any relationship, it is just as important to be right with the person as to be right in the argument. Sometimes it is even more important. My wife and I might disagree about roles or responsibilities. We might get into an argument over who was supposed to call the pest control (but failed to). In the end, however, I would much rather be right with my wife than be proven right in the argument. Of course, there are times when being right in the argument is important. If a glass on the table contains either strychnine or lemonade, it is vitally important to know who is right. But even then, I don't want my wife to drink the strychnine just to prove me right! Sometimes in ministry, it is easy to become so frustrated with people that a minister would rather them leave the church or be excluded from the ministry rather than disagree with them. This is a danger to the soul of the minister!

The work of the ministry is the formation of men, women, and children into the image of Christ by the power of the Spirit. Having committed yourself to this spiritual work, you can give up trying to be the catalyst for someone's spiritual formation, and instead focus on faithfulness to the task of disciple-making.

There is a saying among sound educators: "Teach the student, not the subject." Of course, in the Christian life we see Jesus as the ultimate teacher. God is the one ultimately who informs us and teaches us Truth. But the task of the minister, in making disciples from all nations, is to teach the truth of the gospel to those disciples. Teaching people in the church happens best within the context of relationships. It may be easy in larger churches for the pastor to be primarily a preacher to a group of people he hardly knows, but in the vast majority of churches the pastor is teaching people with whom he must have relationships. Additionally, for teaching to be *transformative* and not merely *informative* the minister should build relationships with church members.

Ministers are not simply subject-matter experts who pass along information to their students. Rather, ministers instruct Christians in the way of Christian life and practice. Yes, ministers summarize and explain the truths of the Christian faith, things like doctrine and biblical understanding. But the ignorance ministers seem to battle is ignorance of God, not merely ignorance of truths about God. Because the purpose of disciple-making is the spiritual formation of the believer, ministers are teaching Christ and his way of life. Training those in our ministries to live as followers of Jesus is more complicated and more difficult than merely teaching them the principles of Christian theology. We are striving to help women and men learn to follow Christ and embody his way of life in their own relationships. For that to happen, they need to see that way of life expressed in our own relationships with them. Church members learn how to participate in the wonder of the gospel by sharing in life together with other Christians. Pastors are tasked with helping create an environment for that participation to occur.

That is not to say that increased membership is the sign of fruitfulness or faithfulness. By making church ministry about numbers, ministers set themselves up for frustration and disappointment if artificial goals are not met. But focusing solely on the care of people's souls can bring significant refreshment into the lives of ministers.

Understanding Ministry as People-Focused

The pastoral calling to minister to real people in real settings in the real world shapes how we think about ourselves in relation to people. Computer programmers, engineers, and mechanics recognize that they are focused on *things* rather than people. That is not to say there is not a component of their jobs that require some level of skill with people, but the job they are performing is ultimately about writing good code, constructing a bridge, or repairing a broken motor. For pastors, the job is ultimately about *people* rather than things. Success in ministry is not judged according to the size of the church's building, program metrics, sermon production, or even attendance at worship services. Instead, success is measured in the transformation of people into mature disciples of Jesus Christ. There are four foundational categories of our relationships with people on which we can build a lasting and fruitful ministry.

Servant Leadership

First, ministry is characterized by *servant leadership.* In John 13:1–17, Jesus modeled a ministry grounded in being a servant to others. The pastor is both a model to the congregation of this type of servanthood and the one responsible for helping lead the congregation into service to one another. By following the model of Jesus, the pastor sees himself first and foremost as a servant and never a master. Moreover, he sees the people in his congregation as those whom he is called to serve. It is often difficult to serve difficult people, but the wise pastor recognizes that he is not above the people he is serving. Additionally, his faithful service to the congregation is the manner by which he leads them to become servants as well.

As the Good Shepherd, Jesus lays down his life for the sheep (John 10:11). As shepherds to a flock, ministers follow this example in their congregation by embodying sacrificial and servant-hearted leadership. The metaphor of the shepherd emphasizes the relational nature of the pastor's calling to care, guide, and personally invest in the lives of the people in the church.

Shared Ministry

A second characteristic of people-focused ministry is practicing a *shared ministry.* Every member of the church has a unique and important role to play in the broader ministry of the church (1 Corinthians 12). As a spiritual leader in the congregation, the pastor is tasked with helping men and women discover their role and empowering them to fulfill that role faithfully. Leading a church in practicing a shared ministry, where the pastor and the congregation build one another up in the gospel, care for one another, and minister to one another, prevents the pastor from being overwhelmed by the needs of the congregation, and facilitates spiritual growth among the entire congregation.

Great Commission Focus

A third characteristic of people-focused ministry is an *emphasis on the Great Commission.* In Matt 28:18–20, Jesus instructs his disciples to "go and make disciples of me from all nations." The church has been commissioned to this goal of disciple-making, which begins with the all-important task of evangelism. The church's mission to proclaim the gospel to people who are not Christians is vital to faithful ministry. As a spiritual leader, the pastor leads the congregation in participation in this mission to *people.* Churches do not evangelize cities or neighborhoods or geographical areas; churches evangelize people. Helping the congregation to learn to have gospel conversations with people in their city, their neighborhood, or their geographical area is a necessary part of the pastor's job.[1] The Great Commission is a call to relational ministry through engaging with people with the gospel of Jesus Christ.

---

[1] See our book *Sharing Jesus without Freaking Out,* 2nd ed., for more on evangelism by people to people through gospel conversations.

In the Great Commission, Jesus instructs his disciples to bring new believers into the life and ministry of the church through baptism. Once a part of the church, these new disciples are taught to follow Christ, grow in him, and share in his ministry. Disciple-making is not complete when someone becomes a Christian, because being a disciple of Jesus means participating in the shared ministry of the church to serve others and proclaim to them the gospel of Jesus.

Pastors do not merely disseminate information. They do not fulfill their ministry solely through helping people know true things, even true things about God. Instead, they are disciple-makers whose purpose is to help people know the Truth, to know God himself. Pastors invest in the lives of people to help them know Jesus, grow in Jesus, and show Jesus to other people.

Living in Community

A final characteristic of people-focused ministry is *living as the Body of Christ.* Churches are not a collection of individual Christians each striving on their own to be the best Christians possible. Sometimes we imagine the Christian as an individual spiritual athlete competing alongside other Christians but without any real organic connection with them. Paul's use of the analogy of an athlete is not meant to imply we are disconnected from one another, but rather to illustrate the importance of training, giving effort, and focusing on the goal in our Christian lives. But that striving for Christian living is done within the Christian community. The church is an interconnected and interdependent community of disciples of Jesus. The pastor is tasked with nurturing this sense of community, helping people learn to minister to and care for one another. The "one another" commands of the New Testament represent a comprehensive picture of what the church as the Body of Christ looks like. Whether forgiving one another, bearing one another's burdens, or praying for one another, the Christian as the builder of community best captures the essence of the church's life as God intends it. Knowing that the pastor's job is to lead the congregation into greater mutual service as a body of believers can ensure a laser focus on people as the product of ministry rather than programming as the product.

Ministry Is Ultimately about Relationships

Having seen the characteristics of people-focused ministry, we can now explore the relational nature of the pastor's ministry. The relationship between pastors and members of the church is not just important, it is the essence of the ministry itself. Pastors may often see the tasks associated with ministry in isolation from the relationships that comprise the church and the church's ministry. It is important to recognize the relational nature of ministry in order to remain focused on the calling at hand.

As we saw previously, the term *pastor* is a translation of the word for *shepherd.* The metaphor of the minister as shepherd emphasizes the relational nature of the pastor's function. As a shepherd, the pastor guides, protects, and cares for the sheep. Those aspects of the ministry can easily be overlooked. The pastor's job is to care for people the same way a shepherd cares for sheep. Ministers need relationships with members of their flock that enable them to know, lead, and nurture the Christians under their care. The pastor guides the congregation to green pastures and still waters. He protects the congregation from harmful teaching, to be sure, but also from harmful attitudes and actions. By living in this type of relationship with his congregation, the pastor can know, lead, and protect the spiritual well-being of the church. Whether in preaching, teaching, planning, or leading, the pastor must recognize that he is acting towards his congregation as a shepherd acts towards his sheep.

Providing spiritual nurture and care requires the pastor to have genuine relationships with people in the church. Shepherds cannot care for sheep while on the other side of the mountain. Pastors who do not "smell like sheep" are probably not practicing relational ministry. This type of genuine relationship exhibits itself in a variety of ways. Pastoral care for those in the congregation requires the minister to provide emotional and practical support to people along with spiritual guidance. This does not mean that pastors should expect themselves, or be expected by others, to have all the knowledge required to help people with every problem. Instead, the pastor has to be "with" members of the congregation in their times of sickness, hurt, pain, and loss. Pastors are necessarily good counselors for emotional or financial problems, but an uncaring pastor who cannot walk alongside a church member during times of distress will probably suffer from strained or broken relationships in ministry. And because ministry is inherently relational, where there is a broken or strained relationship, there is probably not much room for disciple-making. It is hard for a pastor to disciple a church member with whom there is little love or genuine concern. Pastors must learn to be "present" during times of joy and times of sadness, as that presence becomes the basis for relational ministry.

Because the pastor is a disciple-maker, he is always striving to invest in the spiritual growth and maturation of church members. But this disciple-making requires the pastor to walk alongside individuals as they navigate complex and sometimes difficult lives. How does one live as a Christian when facing loss? Discipleship happens in the real world, so the pastor has to be present in that world with his congregation. Pastors are investing in the lives of their church members, offering them guidance and encouragement. They are leading the call to "spur one another on to love and good deeds" (Heb 10:24 NIV).

Pastors also should be seen living the Christian life themselves. A pastor standing in the pulpit can appear to be any type of Christian he wants to appear to be. Church members can hear about discipleship from the pulpit, but they also need to see it lived out. Paul tells Timothy to be an example of the Christian life (1 Tim 4:12). Presence with people allows the pastor to minister to them, but it also allows the pastor to model for people the type of Christian he is teaching them to become. We cannot overstate the importance of living life with the congregation. Discipleship is inherently relational both in its goal (people who grow as Christians) and in its means (people discipling people).

When pastors practice this time of relational ministry, it enables them to build authentic Christian community in the church. Pastors play an indispensable role in fostering a sense of community in the church. Beyond establishing programs and producing events, their ministry promotes fellowship, encourages mutual service, and creates opportunities for connectedness in the church. By developing a sense of authentic Christian community, the pastor helps the church create a place for Christians to experience the presence of the Spirit of God who nurtures their souls and forms them into mature followers of Jesus. As Christians grow in their relationships with God and with one another, they in turn share in the work of the ministry and the progress of the gospel more fully, living as brothers and sisters in the family of God.

How to Handle Relational Challenges

At the core of all healthy relationships is open and honest communication. Being proactive in communication with people is the starting place. My wife and I talk to one another every day about any number of topics. We do not wait for problems to arise before we communicate. We talk about the places we went as well as the places we want to go. We talk about our kids, our jobs, our friends, and our feelings. Conversations are the key for relationships. And then, when there is a challenge we encounter, we already have the foundation for dealing with that challenge together as a team. The same thing must be true in the church. Your relationships with those to whom you are ministering does not begin at the point of conflict or when a challenge arises. Your relationship precedes the challenge, and how you manage your relationship before conflict often determines what the outcome of that challenge to your relationship will be.

There are some ways you can be proactive in your communication with people in your ministry that will help strengthen your relationship with them. First, be open about *why* you do what you do. Misunderstandings are at the root of a lot of conflict. If you regularly share with your congregation why you do the things you do, you provide a foundation for them to consider when they have questions. Explain your perception of how you see your role with people, whether individually or in group settings. Ask trusted men and women in the church if they see your purpose in the same way you do. Do not be afraid to say, "This is how I see my job. Do you see it that way?" That corresponds to a husband and wife saying, "Here's how I see my role. Do you agree?" Proactive communication about why you do what you do goes a long way in preventing problems.

Second, learn to ask questions about how people are growing in their faith. Sometimes the relational challenges we face in ministry are unrelated to our actual job. Assess your work in disciple-making by asking people how they see their own maturity in Christ. Do not rush to give them your assessment; instead, ask them to assess themselves. Spiritual conversations turn the attention away from ourselves to the work of the gospel. Because your job is to see the progress of the gospel in their lives, center your conversations around the gospel as much as possible.

Third, be an encourager. Paul writes to encourage the hearts of his readers. Be someone who encourages people in your congregation. Life is hard. People are rarely appreciated in life. Their boss may not encourage them. Their spouses may not encourage them. They certainly do not need their pastor to not encourage them either. As Hebrews instructs, encourage people to love and good works (Heb 10:24). Because the church is a family, and as the pastor you are to be leading in spiritual growth, be the older sibling who is the younger sibling's biggest cheerleader. Celebrate victories and console them after defeats. Cheer them on to godly living. Acknowledge when people choose wisely. Positive reinforcement in the work of the ministry can help establish a healthy environment for your work as a disciple-making leader in the church. Pastoral ministry involves encouraging younger Christians and older Christians alike to love Jesus and love others.

A final encouragement about communication: lead with words and actions. Communicate openly and honestly with people, but also demonstrate what you intend to communicate through faithful ministry. Telling people you love them without actually loving them is not ministry. If people really are the ministry, then model how they ought to treat one another through your actions toward them. Love them, pray for them, encourage them, bless them, care for them, and bear their burdens. And do so in an environment of authentic Christian community. Do not just try to lead people to be the Body of Christ, show them what it means to be the Body of Christ.

The Fruit of Prioritizing People in Ministry

By focusing on people rather than programming, you will be able to mitigate many of the root causes of burnout we have seen throughout the book. Pastors who see people as a means to an end rather than as the intended purpose of ministry may end up frustrated, bitter, lonely, and even out of ministry. But ministers who understand the people-focused nature of the Great Commission and devote themselves to a ministry dedicated to helping people grow in their relationship with Jesus and with one another will be able to participate in a fruitful and enjoyable ministry. What are some key elements of such a faithful ministry?

Disciple-Making Disciples

When you view people as the ministry, you are able to devote yourselves to making disciples who themselves become disciple-makers. If people are just cogs in a system of ministry programs, they will never become reproducing Christians. As Christians grow in their faith, however, they become increasingly enthusiastic about the things of God and the work of the ministry. They mature in their faith. Alternatively, when Christians are not maturing into leaders who are committed to the Great Commission and the progress of the gospel, they will see themselves as workers on an assembly line. Labor leads to burden. Burden leads to frustration and discontentment. Discontentment leads to unmet expectations and conflict. Conflict leads to burnout. By focusing on the spiritual growth of people in your ministry, you can help them avoid their own burnout and help mitigate the causes of burnout for you as well. As you build authentic relationships with people in your ministry, they become evangelists themselves and take seriously the disciple-making mission of which they are a part.

Healthy Community

1 Corinthians 12 speaks of each member of the body fulfilling their own role for the common good. Focusing on people in your own ministry helps them fulfill the ministry to which they have been called. That ministry establishes a healthy community of believers who are loving one another, caring for one another, and acting interdependently with one another for the sake of the gospel and the glory of God. When the church is healthy, its members express genuine concern for one another, including their pastors. Such an encouraging community of faith creates a sense of enthusiasm for the ministry that permeates the relationships within the church, which also extends to the surrounding community as people live their lives at work, at school, and in their neighborhood.

Conclusion

While the temptation to spend time on "easy" church tasks such as planning and programming is significant, failure to focus on authentic relationships within the church as the means to making disciples is a recipe for frustration and failure. Ministry requires caring for people the way a shepherd cares for sheep—being present, being truthful, being open, being genuine. The goal of ministry is faithfulness in making disciples of people—real people, in the real world.

Ministering to people can be wearisome. The frustrations of trying to care for people who often do not want your care, do not value your ideas, and do not always accept your goals for their lives can be overwhelming. While relationships with people can be a source of consternation, those relationships are the only bridge you have to helping them mature as disciples of Jesus Christ. In order to avoid the burnout that comes from broken relationships and frustrations related to people, we have to dedicate ourselves to the constant refrain, "The people are the ministry."

Ministry is not the programming, the systems, the facilities, the sermons, the calendar, or any host of other distractions from the main purpose of our service: people. Beyond the day-to-day administrative and other ministry tasks, the core of Christian ministry is the relationships between the shepherd and the flock. As ministers we strive to help people hear the gospel, learn to study their Bibles, discover the Christian life, grow in their relationships with one another, forgive those who have sinned against them, and care for the widow and orphan. In the end, as ministers we are working with people. Whatever programs we devise, their purpose is to help people. We construct facilities to give people a place to gather. We write and deliver sermons and Bible studies so that people can grow in Christ. Ministers are in the people business. And by remembering that important reality, we can shape our ministry around the goal of seeing people grow in Christ so that the personal and relational frustrations we face do not lead us to burnout.

Eight-Week Challenge

The Eight-Week Challenge allows individuals, small groups, and college/seminary classrooms to interact with the teaching and principles found in *Serving Jesus without Burning Out.*

The purpose of the challenge is to answer the questions: So now what? Now that I know the danger areas and concerns related to burning out and not finishing ministry well, what can I do next?

In this eight-week challenge, we want to personalize the lessons learned in each chapter. Our goal is for you to know how to do ministry with a healthier outlook and way of life at the end of these eight weeks.

We created these weekly challenges for ordinary people with busy lives. You can think deeply about your life and ministry in a few minutes each day—first thing in the morning, over lunch, or at night before bed. Be patient with yourself as you work through the next eight weeks. This book highlights some common areas of concern that lead to burnout. For many readers, these challenges will push you to replace old patterns of thought and behavior.

As Paul wrote in Phil 1:6, "I am sure of this, that he who started a good work in you will carry it on to completion until the day of Christ Jesus."

Each section is designed around three simple activities. Take some time each week to work through as much as you can. Don't just answer these questions in your head; record your insights in a notebook or on a computer document.

1. *Scripture Meditation.* Take time to think about the scripture passages at the beginning of each week. Consider how they apply to the challenge presented in each chapter. If possible, commit these passages to memory.
2. *Application.* Work through several questions each day. Keep a journal and record your growth.
3. *Prayer.* Spend several minutes each day praying through the different topics provided.

Our hope for success is not in the words or ideas presented in this book. Instead, we trust that the God who called us into this ministry will sustain us. Let's begin this eight-week challenge by committing our efforts to the Lord.

Heavenly Father,

This ministry is yours and I am your servant. My heart desires to honor you each day of my life. I want to finish well, but I will need your help.

Use these exercises to help me overcome the temptations that could lead me to bad decisions, poor thinking, and unhealthy lifestyles.

Most importantly, lead me to yourself through the journey. My hope is summarized in Paul's words to the Philippians believers: To know you and the power of your resurrection and the fellowship of your sufferings, being conformed to your death,

Amen

Week 1

Principle: Ministry is a different type of vocation with unique challenges.

Scriptures for Meditation:

And he himself gave some to be apostles, some prophets, some evangelists, some pastors and teachers, to equip the saints for the work of ministry, to build up the body of Christ, until we all reach unity in the faith and in the knowledge of God's Son, growing into maturity with a stature measured by Christ's fullness. (Eph 4:11–13)

May our Lord Jesus Christ himself and God our Father, who has loved us and given us eternal encouragement and good hope by grace, encourage your hearts and strengthen you in every good work and word. (2 Thess 2:16–17)

Questions for Reflection and Application

1. Write down a list of fears you have about ministry. Reflect on the root of each of those fears. Do they have anything in common? Seek to explain why these concern you.
2. How do you deal with conflict with other people? What steps do you take to deescalate that conflict?
3. Write down these areas of potential (or actual) conflict in ministry and explain ways to address them.
4. Do you ever feel unqualified for ministry due to your weaknesses? How do you respond to those weaknesses?

5. Spend time in prayer specifically asking God to encourage you and strengthen you for the good work of ministry. Focus time in prayer on your dependence on God for His strength.

Week 2

Principle: You did not choose the job, the job chose you.

Scriptures for Meditation:

Therefore, since we have this ministry because we were shown mercy, we do not give up. Instead, we have renounced secret and shameful things, not acting deceitfully or distorting the word of God, but commending ourselves before God to everyone's conscience by an open display of the truth. But if our gospel is veiled, it is veiled to those who are perishing. In their case, the god of this age has blinded the minds of the unbelievers to keep them from seeing the light of the Gospel of the glory of Christ, who is the image of God. For we are not proclaiming ourselves but Jesus Christ as Lord, and ourselves as your servants for Jesus's sake. (2 Cor 4:1–5)

And he himself gave some to be apostles, some prophets, some evangelists, some pastors and teachers, to equip the saints for the work of ministry, to build up the body of Christ, until we all reach unity in the faith and in the knowledge of God's Son, growing into maturity with a stature measured by Christ's fullness. (Eph 4:11–13)

Questions for Reflection and Application

1. How did God call you into ministry? Spend a few minutes and jot down the high spots of this monumental event. Don't forget to consider the internal and external means of validation.

2. Has there ever been a moment when God's call served as motivation for you to face hardships and temptations?
3. What hardships and temptations are you facing today? Spend some time in prayer, meditate on God's call, and ask him to give you endurance and conviction to persevere.
4. How can the reminder, "You didn't choose this ministry; it chose you," give you hope in your current ministry?
5. Spend half a day in prayer. Ask the Lord to give you *his* vision for your current ministry assignment. Talk about this with your spouse, ministry team, or a trusted friend. Ask them to pray that you can keep this vision before you.

Week 3

Principle: You are the perfect person for your ministry.

Scripture for Meditation:

But Moses replied to the Lord, "Please, Lord, I have never been eloquent—either in the past or recently or since you have been speaking to your servant—because my mouth and my tongue are sluggish." The Lord said to him, "Who placed a mouth on humans? Who makes a person mute or deaf, seeing or blind? Is it not I, the Lord*? Now go! I will help you speak and I will teach you what to say." Moses said, "Please, Lord, send someone else."* (Exod 4:10–13)

Questions for Reflection and Application

1. Write down a list of unique aspects to your personality; describe yourself as you think you are.
2. What activities in life truly give you a sense of joy and satisfaction? Can any of those help indicate ways you can minister to other people?
3. If there is any weakness that would prevent you from doing ministry, what would that be? How can God use you because of that weakness and not despite it?
4. Take time this week for a spiritual renewal:
    a. Read Psalm 119 aloud.
    b. Read the book of Philippians aloud.

c. Make a list of as many people as you can who you know are not Christians. Do not rush this. Pray for each person by name.

Week 4

Principle: Faithful ministry requires ongoing growth

Scriptures for Meditation:

I am the vine; you are the branches. The one who remains in me and I in him produces much fruit, because you can do nothing without me. (John 15:5)

The Lord is my shepherd; I have what I need.
He lets me lie down in green pastures; he leads me beside quiet waters.
He renews my life; he leads me along the right paths for his name's sake. (Pss 23:1–3)

Questions for Reflection and Application

1. Reflect on your growth or drift over the past several months or years.
   a. Where are you experiencing life in a rut or drift?
   b. What are the consequences you are enduring because of this lack of growth?
2. Look at your bookshelf (paper or ebook). What books do you own but have not read? Make a plan to read these books over the next several months.
3. Spend 30 minutes meditating on Ps 139:14 (and other verses that come to mind). Thank God for your physical health. Ask him to keep your body strong and ready for the challenges of ministry.

4. Set aside time for a half-day spiritual retreat:
    a. Begin by reading a chapter from the OT, NT, and 3 Psalms
    b. Spend time in praise and thanksgiving
    c. Spend time confessing sin and receiving God's forgiveness
    d. Spend time praying for your family, church, ministry, and missionaries
    e. Pray for yourself.
        i. Are you nearing burnout?
        ii. Are you frustrated with the Lord or your ministry?
        iii. Lay out your hopes and dreams for ministry.
    f. Close by slowly praying through the Lord's prayer, meditating and expanding each phrase

Week 5

Principle: Guard your character, it is the only message you have.

Scripture for Meditation:

For our struggle is not against flesh and blood, but against the rulers, against the authorities, against the cosmic powers of this darkness, against evil, spiritual forces in the heavens. For this reason take up the full armor of God, so that you may be able to resist in the evil day, and having prepared everything, to take your stand. (Eph 6:12–13)

Questions for Reflection and Application

1. Be honest with yourself: what is the biggest temptation to sin that you face?
2. What is the struggle you have that, if people discovered that sin, they would question your qualification for ministry?
3. What sin(s) that you struggle with would damage the reputation of your church or your message if you committed said sin?
4. Reflect on practical steps you are taking to avoid committing those sins and damaging your reputation as a Christian and a minister. Write those steps down.
5. God has given you his spirit so you can obey him. Pray through your temptations, confess your sins, and ask God for his grace and strength.

Week 6

Principle: The Sabbath was made for man, not man for the Sabbath.

Scriptures for Meditation:

"*Come to me, all of you who are weary and burdened, and I will give you rest. Take up my yoke and learn from me, because I am lowly and humble in heart, and you will find rest for your souls. For my yoke is easy and my burden is light.*" (Matt 11:28–30)

Do not have other gods besides me. Do not make an idol for yourself, whether in the shape of anything in the heavens above or on the earth below or in the waters under the earth. Do not bow in worship to them, and do not serve them; for I, the Lord your God, am a jealous God . . . (Exod 20:3–5)

Their idols are silver and gold, made by human hands. They have mouths but cannot speak, eyes, but cannot see. They have ears but cannot hear, noses, but cannot smell. They have hands but cannot feel, feet, but cannot walk. They cannot make a sound with their throats. Those who make them are just like them, as are all who trust in them. (Pss 115:4–8)

Questions for Reflection and Application

1. In what ways are your identity, hope, joy, purpose, and spirituality linked to your ministry? Do you think you are in danger of making ministry your idol?

2. Spend 30 minutes meditating on the meaning of Sabbath. Make sure not to neglect that Christ is your ultimate Sabbath.
3. Open a blank document (digital or paper). Fill the paper by answering these sentence prompts:
   a. I am so tired in . . .
   b. I am so tired of . . .
   c. I need to bring _____ to Jesus and find rest.
4. Plan one day and completely vacate from work. Concentrate on the Lord, your family, and your rest.

Week 7

Principle: Leadership is a lonely path, but you were never intended to do it alone.

Scriptures for Meditation:

Brothers and sisters, if someone is overtaken in any wrongdoing, you who are spiritual, restore such a person with a gentle spirit, watching out for yourselves so that you also won't be tempted. Carry one another's burdens; in this way, you will fulfill the law of Christ. (Gal 6:1–2)

How delightfully good when brothers live together in harmony!
It is like fine oil on the head, running down on the beard,
running down Aaron's beard onto his robes.
It is like the dew of Hermon falling on the mountains of Zion.
For there the Lord has appointed the blessing— life forevermore.
(Ps 133)

Questions for Reflection and Application

1. Quick—If you were in trouble or facing significant temptation, who would you call for help?
   a. Are you comfortable with your answer?
   b. What does your answer tell you about the health of your friendships?
2. Reverse question 1. Who would call you if they were in trouble or faced significant temptation?
   a. Do they know they could call you?

   b. How can you ensure others know you are willing to be a "friend in need?"
3. Which practical steps for making friends will you reasonably practice? Make plans to take the first step.
4. Create a prayer list for your friends. On an index card (digital or paper):
   a. Write their name
   b. Write out one scripture verse that captures your Godward hope for them.
   c. Write out 1–3 specific prayers.
   d. Set time to pray regularly for your friends and let them know you are praying.

Week 8

Principle: Ministry is about people, be honest about your humanity.

Scripture for Meditation:

Now there are different gifts, but the same Spirit. There are different ministries, but the same Lord. And there are different activities, but the same God works all of them in each person. A manifestation of the Spirit is given to each person for the common good. (1 Cor 12:4–7)

Questions for Reflection and Application

1. Make a list of people in your life who are a blessing to you. Stop and thank God for them.
2. Make a list of people in your life who cause you frustration or anger. Stop and thank God for them as well, asking God to show you how even the frustration of dealing with them can serve your formation as a minister.
3. How well do you deal with people who disagree with you or actively oppose your wishes? Would your spouse or best friend agree with your assessment?
4. This week, meet with someone you trust. Ask them to assess your strengths and weakness in relationships with other people. Then take their assessment to heart.

General Index

A

Aaron, 118, 185
Abednego, 51, 118, 136
Abraham, 44, 50
abuse, 61
accolades, 88, 105–6, 131
accomplishment, sense of, 73
accountability, 4–5, 96–97, 146
Adam and Eve, 144
adultery, 21
affirmation, external, 45
American culture, 145
Andronicus, 14
anger, xvi, xxi, 43, 96, 135, 145, 187
anxiety, 24, 128
apostle, role of, 13–15
appreciation, 65
atonement, 130
authenticity, 55–58, 109–10. *See also* inauthenticity
availability, xvii, 65
avoidance, 103. *See also* laziness

B

Babel, Tower of, 105
Baggins, Frodo, 137–38. *See also* friendship; Gamgee, Samwise
baptism, 71, 161
Barnabas, 14
Bible intake, 92
bitterness, xxi, 64, 70, 114. *See also* envy
Blackaby, Henry, 33–34
Blomberg, Craig, 128
body of Christ, the, 7, 17, 20, 100, 161–62, 167, 173, 175
burnout, definition of, 2
busyness, 48

C

call, of God. *See chapter 2, "The Sustaining Power of Your Call"* (31–54)
call, universal, 34–36
care, reciprocal, 8
celebrity, 64, 106
Chambers, Oswald, 33, 36
Chapman, Stephen Curtis, 154
charisma, 23, 73
Christlikeness, 90, 92
Chrysostom, John, 42–43
communication, xvii, xxi, 165–67
communion, 10–11
comparison. *See chapter 3, "Being God's Servant Where You Are, As You Are"* (55–76)
confirmation, 45, 68
conflict, interpersonal, 37, 48
contentedness, 69
conviction, internal, 45
courage, 90, 148
covenant, new, 12
creativity, 85, 94, 103
crisis, 3, 33, 37, 124, 141
criticism, xxi, xxii, 38, 43, 141, 145
culture shock, 32
curiosity, 83, 145

D

danger, xvi, xx, 16, 51, 82, 89, 97, 107, 110, 119, 123, 125, 146, 153–54, 156, 171, 183
Daniel (prophet), 51
Dark Knight, 145–46
David (king), 51, 134, 146
deacon, xiv, 11, 25. *See also diakonos*
decisions, unhealthy, 1–2
deconversion, 2, 57
depression, 24, 146
despair, 72
devotion, 24, 119, 121
diakonos, 11–12
disability, 61–62. *See also* Ritchie, Daniel
disciple, 65, 67, 73–74, 88, 106, 114–15, 126–28, 141, 148, 157–58, 160–61, 163, 168–70
discipleship, 50, 164
disciplines, spiritual, 90–93
discontentment, 108, 168
dishonesty, 56, 64, 68
disillusionment, 7, 69, 100
doubts, xvii, 57, 127, 152
drift, the, 80–82, 97
duty, 22, 48, 66, 102, 108, 119

E

emptiness, 89, 91, 121, 128

endurance, 33, 115, 130–31, 176
enthusiasm, 90, 131, 168–69
envy, 64, 72, 75–76, 107–8. *See also* bitterness; discontentment
Epaphras, 12
Epaphroditus, 13–14, 44
Ephesus, church in, 133
equanimity, 148
ethics. *See* morality
evangelism, 9, 91, 100, 103, 160
evangelist, 7, 13, 15–16, 20, 168, 173, 175
exhaustion, xiv, xv, xix, 2, 78, 128
  and drift, 81
  and finishing well, 48
  paralyzing, 2
  and performance, 64
  relational, 141
  and rest, 127–28
  season of, 138
  and secret sin, 101
  and workaholism, 120
experience, mystical, 45

F

failure, moral, 2, 7, 24, 48, 146. *See also* adultery; greed; hypocrisy; immorality; pride; sexual sin
famine, 12
fasting, 92
fatigue, 96, 101
favoritism, 141
feedback, xvi, 110
fellowship, 28, 34, 92, 139, 142–43, 151, 165, 172
fidelity, 18, 21, 67
food pyramid, 86
forgiveness, 35, 113–14, 180
formation, spiritual, xvi, 4, 23, 88–92, 101, 110, 157
The Four Spiritual Laws, 100
friendship, xix, xx, 4–5, 97, 138–44, 146, 149–54, 185. *See also* Baggins, Frodo; Gamgee, Samwise
Frodo. *See* Baggins, Frodo
fruit, spiritual, 24, 75, 104
frustration
  and authenticity, 69
  and comparison, 64
  and confirmation, 45
  and conflict, 37
  and friendship, 154
  and God's call, 53
  and growth, 78
  of John the Baptist, 127
  and loneliness, 148
  and metrics, 158
  and rest, 127
  and service, 19, 28, 102, 116, 156, 168–69
fun, 94, 154

G

Gamgee, Samwise, 137, 139, 144. *See also* Baggins, Frodo; friendship
Garland, David, 37, 39
George, Timothy, 143, 148
Gideon, 44
giftedness, 24, 26, 59
glory of God, 8, 36, 169
godliness, 18, 80, 92, 96, 100, 108, 150
golden calf, 118. *See also* Aaron
Golden Rule, the, 149
gratification
  instant, 93
  selfish, 104–5
gratitude, 76
Great Commission, the, 10, 15, 20, 50, 65, 73, 160–61, 168
greed, 145
growth. *See chapter 4, "Lifelong Growth for Lifelong Ministry"* (77–97)

H

habits, 3–5, 126
hardships, 40, 90, 130, 176
health, physical, 86–87, 95–96, 101–2, 179
hero, 56, 84, 145
holiness, personal, 4, 49, 89
honesty, 115, 140
hostility, 40, 91
humiliations, 40
humility, xxi, xxii, 66, 109, 111–12, 133
hypocrisy, 23–24, 67, 108–9

I

identity, 56, 59–63, 68, 119–22, 124, 126–28, 183
idolatry. *See chapter 6, "Workaholics Don't Die Winners; They Die Empty"* (117–36)
ignorance, xi, 36, 40, 157
illness, 7, 32, 63, 96, 154, 163
image of Christ, 10, 156
image of God, 31, 60–61, 129–30, 175
imitation, 58
immorality, 21–22, 24, 104–5. *See also* failure: moral
inadequacy, sense of, 59
inauthenticity, 56. *See also* authenticity
Indiana Jones, 118
infidelity, 64
ingenuity, 24, 73
injustice, 114
insecurity, 50, 141
integrity, 108, 115
Isaiah, 44, 51
isolation, xix, xx, 141, 146–47, 152–53, 162

J

Jeremiah, 51–52, 119
Jethro, 147–48
Joab, 146
John the Baptist, 82, 105, 126
Jonah, 135
Jonathan, 146
Joshua, 51
Junia, 14
justice, 113, 146

K

Keller, Tim, 118–19
kindness, 66, 106, 112
King Kong, 118
knowledge of God, 7, 41–43, 85, 173, 175

L

law of Christ, the, 137, 142, 148–49, 185
laziness. *See also* avoidance; leisure
- intellectual, 85
- in ministry, 102–4
- physical, 96
- and workaholism, 122

Lea, Thomas, 49
leisure, 101–4
lifestyle, sedentary, 87
Lifeway Research, 139
Lifeway Voices, 78
loneliness, xix, xx, 139, 146–47, 152–53
longevity, 5, 22, 59, 78, 85, 96, 147
Lord of the Rings, 137
Lord's Prayer, the, 113, 144, 180
love language, 65
lust, 145
Luther, Martin, 40

M

malaise, 85
manipulation, 104, 125
Martha, 11
Matthew (apostle), 51, 126
maturity, 7, 10, 23, 58, 61, 173, 175
- and authenticity, 57–58
- and change, 70
- and imitation, 68, 108
- intellectual, 97
- reading for, 94
- spiritual, 23, 26, 89, 93, 109–10, 115, 141, 166
- and spiritual disciplines, 91–93
- as ultimate purpose, 60–61

M'Cheyne, Robert Murray, 49, 86, 96
meaninglessness, 33, 128
meditation, 92
mercy, 31, 40, 45, 66, 113, 175
Meshach, 51, 118, 136
ministry collapse, 1, 3

mission, of the church
  [p.10-, 20 ("mission to the church")]
missionary, xiii, 10, 32, 36, 44, 60, 105, 123, 146, 150
mission, of the church, 10–11, 13
Mohler, Albert, 93–94
money, love of, 48, 106–7. *See also* greed
morality, 21, 148
Moses
  call of, 44, 50, 55, 63
  and Joshua, 51
  and the law, 118
  leadership of, 147
  warnings of, 119

N

notoriety, 66

O

obedience, 18, 52–53, 124
omnipresence, of Jesus, 50. *See also* presence, of God
Osborne, Grant, 134

P

Pace, Scott, 35–36
parable of the lost son, 134–35
participation with the Spirit, 91, 93
passion, 37, 45, 52, 81, 99
pastor. *See* shepherd
patience, 19–20, 33, 40, 114–15, 152, 171
pedigree, 33
Pentecost, 15
performance, xxii, 22, 64, 92
persecution, 50, 91
perseverance, 49, 100, 109
personality, 45, 58, 63, 177
Peter (apostle), xviii, 15–16
Peterson, Eugene, 53, 90–91, 125
Pharaoh, 44, 50
Pharisees, 90, 112
Philip, 16. *See also* evangelist
poverty, 107
power
  of the drift, 97
  of the flesh, 73
  of God, 39
  of idolatry, 118
  proper, 43
  pursuit of, 48, 112
  the Spirit, 57
prayer, 45–46, 91–92, 122, 133, 141, 144, 146, 150–51, 154, 172, 174, 176, 186. *See also* disciplines, spiritual; Lord's Prayer, the
  for other pastors, 150
  personal, 4
  regular, 75, 89

presence, of God, 51, 134. *See also* omnipresence, of Jesus
pretentiousness, 69
pride, 45, 48, 57–58, 66, 72, 75, 103, 111, 145, 148
productivity, 54, 102, 131, 133, 148
progress, of the gospel, 19, 111, 165–66, 168
promise, of God, 39, 50, 129
prophet, 7, 13–16, 44, 51, 134–35, 173, 175. *See also* individual prophets
PTSD, 61
public exposure, 101
purity, 18, 48–49
purposelessness, 9, 48

R

rebellion, 127, 144
rest, proper, 87
resurrection, 10, 35, 122, 130, 172
rhythm, xvi, 3, 47, 81, 128
Ritchie, Daniel, 62

S

Sabbath, 117, 128–30, 183–84
sadness, xv, 118, 164
sanctification, 33, 36, 124
Satan, 100
Saunders, Elizabeth, 47
self-indulgence, 105
selflessness, 105
self-preservation, 34
self-promotion, 34
self-sacrifice, xv, 105
Seneca, 148
sentimentalism, 112
sermon preparation, 103
servant-leader, 17, 27–28
servant leadership, xv, 9, 159
sexual sin, 48
Shadrach, 51, 118, 136
shepherd, 16, 23, 68, 112, 159, 162–63, 169–70, 179
sickness. *See* illness
Silas, 44
silence, 92–93, 117. *See also* solitude
sin. *See chapter 5, "God's Not the Only One with a Plan for You"* (99–116)
skill, 33, 50, 59, 63, 79, 83–84, 100, 158
social media, 43, 58, 71, 78, 86
social unrest (2020), 78
solitude, 93. *See also* silence
spiritual formation. *See* formation, spiritual
Spurgeon, Charles, 52, 88
stability, 82
stagnation, 80, 82
Stedman, Ray, 129

Stoicism. *See* Seneca
stress, 21, 72, 102
success, 48–50, 72, 153, 156, 158
and comparison, 65, 71–72
earthly, 41
as faithfulness, 76, 102
and friendship, 5, 141
and health, 86
and leadership, 46
measurement of, 53–54, 122
and spiritual formation, 88
suicide, 2
survival, 103, 144, 152

T

temptation, 62, 81, 88, 100, 143, 145–46, 149, 169
avoidance of, 79
common, 120
to compare, 74–76
to compete, 58
confrontation of, 152
disqualifying, 48
and fatigue, 96
and ministry collapse, 1
resistance of, 104
to sin, 57
Ten Commandments, the, 119, 128
Timothy
as apostle, 14
as evangelist, 16
as an example, 18, 164
as minister, 12, 17, 19, 33, 40, 48, 52, 57
as missionary, 44
Titus, 44
toil, 47, 127
training, insufficient, 7
trauma, 61, 155
trust, 152, 172, 183, 187
in God, 67, 114, 120
and hypocrisy, 109
in Jesus, 57
in the Spirit, 109
Twelve, the, 14

V

Vacation Bible School, 22
vulnerability, xix, 68, 101, 140, 152

W

wealth, affection for, 106–8
Whitney, Donald, 92
widows, 18, 75, 170
Wilcock, Michael, 131
workaholism. *See chapter 6, "Workaholics Don't Die Winners; They Die Empty"* (117–36)
worth, 34
wrath, of God, 119

Scripture Index

Genesis

1:26–27 *60*
2:18 *148*
11:4 *105*
12 *44, 50*

Exodus

3 *44*
3:12 *50*
4:10–13 *55, 177*
4:11 *63*
18 *147*
18:17–18 *147*
20:3–5 *183*

Numbers

32:23 *56*

Joshua

1:5 *51*

Judges

6 *44*

1 Samuel

2:26 *82*

2 Samuel

11 *146*
11:1–2 *146*

Psalms

23:1–3 *179*
23:4 *51*
51:4 *134*
115:1 *105*
115:4–8 *183*
119 *177*
133 *185*
139:14 *179*

Proverbs

17:17 *142*
18:24 *149*
27:6 *142*
27:9–10 *142*

Ecclesiastes

4:10 *139*

Isaiah

6 *44*

Jeremiah

1:8 *51*
10 *119*
20:9 *52*

Daniel

3 *136*
3:17–18 *136*

Jonah

4:2 *135*

Matthew

3 *127*
6:10 *144*
6:12 *113*
7:12 *149*
7:27 *100*
9:36 *112*
11:3 *127*
11:28–30 *117, 126, 183*
28:17 *50*
28:18–20 *10, 50, 160*
28:20 *50–51*

Mark

10:45 *11, 35*

Luke

1:80 *82*
2:52 *82*
12:32 *16*
15 *132*
15:21 *134*
17:10 *66*
24:47 *35*

John

3:30 *105*
10:11 *159*
10:11–14 *16*
12:2 *12*
13:1–17 *111, 159*
13:34–35 *148*
15 *88, 90–91*
15:5 *77, 88, 179*
15:7 *91*
15:9 *91*
15:10 *91*
15:11 *91*
15:12 *91*
15:18 *91*
16:33 *144*
21:16 *16*

Acts

1:21–25 *14*
2:17 *15*
2:42 *14*
5:42 *17*
6:1–6 *11*
6:4 *12*

11:29 *12*
14 *14*
20:20 *17*
20:24 *12*
21:8 *16*

Romans
1 *119*
6 *145*
12:10 *27*
12:16 *27*
15:14 *27*
16:7 *14*

1 Corinthians
1:9 *34*
1:10–17 *71*
1:26–27 *62*
3:5 *12*
11:1 *18, 68*
12 *26, 74, 159, 169*
12:4–6 *64*
12:4–7 *155, 187*
12:5 *12*
12:7 *59*
12:23–25 *58*
12:31 *69*
13:13 *69*
14:3 *15*
14:4 *15*
14:31 *15*
15:47–49 *61*

2 Corinthians
2:14 *38*
2:14–15 *41*
2:14–17 *38*
2:16 *42*
3:6 *12*
4:1–5 *31, 175*
5:17 *60*
5:18 *12*
5:21 *130*
7:10 *134*
8:4 *12*
8:23 *14*
11:8 *12*
11:28 *89*

Galatians
1:6 *143*
1:8 *143*
2 *xviii*
3:1 *143*
5:13 *27, 35*
5:22–23 *111*
6:1 *82*
6:1–2 *137, 142, 185*
6:2 *148*

Ephesians
2:20 *14*
4 *53, 124*
4:1 *35*
4:2 *27*
4:11 *14–15*

4:11–12 *12–13*
4:11–13 *7, 173, 175*
4:12 *17, 27*
4:32 *113*
5:21 *27*
6:12–13 *99, 181*

Philippians
1:6 *171*
2:3–8 *105*
2:25 *13*
3:14 *5*
4:12 *107*

Colossians
1:7 *12*
1:15 *61*
1:25 *12*
3:10 *61*
3:13 *28*
3:16 *17, 28*

1 Thessalonians
2:6 *14*
2:11–12 *34*
5:13 *28*
5:14 *115*
5:15 *28*

2 Thessalonians
2:16–17 *173*

1 Timothy
1:12–17 *40*
1:16 *33*
2:4 *35*
3:1–7 *108*
3:8–13 *11*
4:6 *12, 17*
4:7 *18*
4:8 *87, 96*
4:11 *18*
4:12 *18, 164*
4:16 *21, 48, 116*
5:3 *18*
5:8 *107*
6:10 *106*

2 Timothy
1:13 *19*
1:18 *12*
2:4 *19*
2:4–7 *53*
2:21 *116*
4:2 *19*
4:5 *16*

Hebrews
4:3 *129*
4:9–11 *129*
10:24 *164, 167*
10:24–25 *115*
12:1 *101*

James
1:14–15 *144*
1:22 *67*

1 Peter

1:22 *27*
4:10–11 *12*
5:2 *16*
5:10–11 *34*

2 Peter

3:9 *114*

1 John

1:7 *28*

Revelation

2 *134*
2:2–5 *131*
2:5 *132*
7:9 *35*